Welcome to the World Heritage City

There are places that somehow manage to get under your skin or work their way into in your heart, even though you don't really know them all that well. Bruges is that kind of place. A warm and friendly place, a place made for people. A city whose history made it great, resulting in a well-deserved classification as a Unesco World Heritage site. As mysterious as in the Middle Ages, unashamedly and fun-lovingly Burgundian. In short, a world city that is also a city of the world – and has been since time immemorial.

In this guide you will discover, experience and enjoy Bruges in all its many different facets. There are five separate chapters.

In **chapter 1**, you will learn everything you need to know to prepare for your visit to Bruges. There is a brief summary of the city's rich past, a list of the ten 'must-see' sights, a summary of the best restaurants, useful tips for fun souvenirs and a mass of practical information, including details of the different options for getting around Bruges and a clear explanation about how best to use the 'Bruges City Card'. This card will allow you to visit many of Bruges' most important sites of interest for free or at a significantly reduced price.

The three inspiring walking routes included in **chapter 2** will take you to all the most beautiful spots in town. The detailed map of the city – which you can simply fold out of the back cover of this guide – will make sure that you don't lose your way. The map also shows the licensed places to stay in Bruges, offering a range of accommodation options that runs from ... hor ...

Chapter 3 tells you all about the cultural life of Bruges: a summary of annual events and a full overview of the city's museums, sites of interest, and all its historic, cultural and religious buildings. Although Bruges cherishes its proud history, the city does not dwell on the past. On the contrary, Bruges is more alive than ever before: its beautiful squares and enchanting canals are the regular backdrop for top-class cultural events. And few cities have such a rich and diverse variety of museums, which contain gems dating from the Flemish Primitives of medieval times to the finest modern art of today. Put simply, Bruges is always an experience – whether your interest is art, chocolate, diamonds or chips!

In Bruges you can dine at a different star-rated restaurant each day or perhaps you would prefer lunch at a trendy bistro, before wandering through the winding cobbled streets of the city? As far as food and drink is concerned, in Bruges you can find the best of all worlds. For centuries the local people have known all the best places to go. These are the places, full of charm and character, which you can read about in **chapter 4**. Restaurants, cafés, shops, parks and squares that all bear the seal of approval: 'loved by the locals'. Five 'new arrivals' to the city will also tell you about their favourite places. If you are staying a bit longer in the region, you may want to explore beyond the city boundaries. **Chapter 5** suggests a number of excursions to the Bruges Ommeland, the coast and the Westhoek. The choice is yours!

Discover Bruges

The highlights of Bruges

The 10 classic places that no one should miss!

Rozenhoedkaai: a living picture postcard

The Rozenhoedkaai links the Belfry to the city's network of canals ('reien'). So perhaps it was inevitable that the quay should become one of the most photogenic locations in all Bruges. In fact, this spot is so special that it is almost impossible not to take a photograph: a living postcard that you can be a part of!

A quiet moment in the Beguinage

(Also see page 76)

Some places are so beautiful that you will have no choice but to feel awe. The Beguinage is such a beauty spot. When you amble through its quiet inner court, its purity will leave you speechless. Therefore take your time and while away along the romantic Minnewater where you will fully enjoy the age-old view.

Burg and City Hall: medieval opulence

(More information on page 90)

The Burg is one of the city's most beautiful squares. For more than six centuries, Bruges has been governed from its 14th-century City Hall, one of the oldest and most venerable in the Low Countries. All this time this remarkable historic building has dominated this majestic square. Nowhere else will you be able to experience the city's wealth and affluence so strongly.

The Flemish Primitives: world famous art from Bruges

(More information on pages 81-82)

Admire the unique and world-famous collection of pictures by the Flemish Primitives in the very city where they were painted. Or do you prefer the groundbreaking contemporary art scene, or perhaps poignant and romantic folklore or majestic town palaces? The Bruges Museums will happily serve all your needs.

Wandering through the old Hansa Quarter

From the 13th to the 15th century, Bruges was an important trading centre at the crossroads between the Hansa cities of Scandinavia, England and Germany (known collectively in those days as the 'Easterners') and the most important commercial regions in France, Spain and Italy. The Spanish traders established themselves at Spaanse Loskaai (Spanish Unloading Quay), while the Easterners sat up shops on the Oosterlingenplein (Easterners' Square). Places where you can still sometimes feel the atmosphere of days long gone by.

⚓ The Canals of Bruges: the city's arteries

Experience the city by following an age-old tradition. Cruising Bruges' canals – the remarkable city arteries – you will discover secret gardens, picturesque bridges and wonderfully beautiful views. Although it sounds incredible, Bruges' loveliest places ooze even more charm when you admire them travelling by boat.

The Church of Our Lady: the centuries-old skyline of Bruges

The Church of Our Lady (Onze-Lieve-Vrouwekerk) is most remarkable for its 122 metre-high brick tower, a tribute to the skill of the city's medieval craftsmen and the second highest tower of its kind in the world. Inside the church you can wonder at the beauty of the 'Madonna with Child', a marble masterpiece sculpted by Michelangelo and guaranteed to leave no visitor unmoved.

🏛 Almshouses: charity frozen in stone

(More information on page 46)

Almshouses are tiny villages within the city's ramparts. That's how these medieval residential courts are best described. Centuries ago they were built out of mortar and charity. Today their picturesque gardens, whitewashed façades and glorious silence are the city's havens of peace par excellence.

14 Concert Hall or Culture with a capital C

(More information on page 93)

This imposing and intriguing culture temple is a beacon of light and provides 't Zand, the square on which it stands, with a unique dynamic all on its own. Inside, there is no elaborate theatrical decoration, but a simple, almost minimalist, auditorium with a 'symphonic' arrangement of chairs. In short, the ideal circumstances in which to enjoy classical concerts, jazz, dance or theatre.

Market Square – a must

If there is only one place you can visit in Bruges, this is it. The Market Square is literally and figuratively the beating heart of the city. The colourful guild houses, the clatter of horses' hooves, the rattling of the carriages and the dominating presence of the Belfry all combine to create a setting of great beauty and charm, which is part medieval and part modern. And if you are feeling energetic, you can still climb the 366 steps of the 83-metre high belfry tower, which will reward you with a spectacular panorama over the city and its surrounding hinterland. The Market is also the home of Historium, a brand-new top attraction that takes you back to the golden days of Bruges in the Middle Ages. The balcony on the first floor has a fine view of the square, with its statues of Jan Breydel and Pieter de Coninck, two of the city's most important historical figures.
(For more information about Historium see also page 83)

History in a nutshell

Water played a crucial role in the birth and development of Bruges. It was at this place that a number of streams converged to form the River Reie, which then flowed northwards towards the coastal plain. Through a series of tidal creeks, the river eventually reached the sea. Little wonder, then, that even as far back as Roman times there was already considerable seafaring activity in this region. This has been proven by the discovery of the remains of two sea-going ships from this period, dating from the second half of the 3rd century or the first half of the 4th century. Even so, it would be another five centuries before the name 'Bruges' first began to appear – the word being a derivative of the old-German word 'brugj', which means 'mooring place'. As the centuries passed, Bruges developed into a commercial centre with its own port.

Its growing importance also resulted in it becoming the main fortified residence of the counts of Flanders, so that from the 11th century onwards the city was not only a prosperous trading metropolis, but also a seat of considerable political power.

Taking off

When the city's direct link with the sea was in danger of silting-up in the 12th century, Bruges went through a period of anxiety. Fortunately, the new water-way of the Zwin brought relief. As a result, Bruges was able to call itself the most important trade centre of North-west Europe in the following century. The world's first Bourse began business. Its financial exchanges took place on a square in front of the premises that belonged to Van der Beurse, a Bruges merchant family. In spite of the typical medieval maladies, from epidemics to political unrest and social inequality, the citizens of Bruges prospered, and soon the city developed a magnet-like radiation. Around 1350 the inner city numbered no fewer than 35.000 inhabitants.

Golden Age

Success continually increased. In the 15th century – Bruges' Golden Age – things improved further when the Royal House of Burgundy took up residence in the city. New luxury goods were produced in abundance, and famous painters such as Jan van Eyck and Hans Memling – the great Flemish Primitives – found their cre-ative niche here. The fine arts flourished, and besides a goodly number of fine churches and unique merchant houses, a monumental town hall was also erected. Bruges' success seemed imperishable.

Decline

The death of the popular Mary of Burgundy in 1482 marked a sudden change of fortune. The relationship between the citizens of Bruges and their lord, the widower Maximilian, turned sour, and his Burgundian court left the city. The international merchants followed. Long centuries of wars and changes of political power took their toll. By the middle of the 19th century Bruges had become an impoverished city. Funnily enough, a novel would turn this wretched tide.

Revival

In Bruges la Morte (1892) Georges Rodenbach aptly describes Bruges as a somewhat sleepy, yet extremely mysterious place. Soon Bruges' magnificent patrimony was rediscovered and her mysterious intimacy turned out to be her greatest asset. This élan gave Zeebrugge a new seaport, whilst Bruges itself carefully took her first touristic steps. Success wasn't long in coming. UNESCO added the medieval city centre to its World Heritage list. The rest is history.

From early settlement to international trade centre   (…-1200)

851   Earliest record of the city
863   Baldwin I takes up residence
      at Burg
1127 Charles the Good, Count of Flanders, is murdered in the Church of
      Saint Donatian; first town rampart;
      first Bruges city charter
1134 Creation of the Zwin that links
      Damme with the sea

Bruges' Golden Age   (1369-1500)

1369 Margaret of Dampierre marries
      Philip the Bold, Duke of Burgundy.
      Beginning of the Burgundian
      period
1384 Margaret succeeds her father
      Louis of Male
1430 Marriage of Duke Philip the
      Good with Isabella of Portugal;
      establishment of the Order of
      the Golden Fleece
1436 Jan van Eyck paints the panel
      *Madonna with Canon Joris van
      der Paele*
1482 Death of Mary of Burgundy after
      a fall from her horse
1488 Maximilian of Austria is locked up
      in Craenenburg House on Markt
      for a few weeks

851   1200   1300   1500

Bruges as the economic capital of Northwest Europe   (1200-1400)

1245 Foundation of the Beguinage
1297 Second town rampart
1302 Bruges Matins and Battle
      of the Golden Spurs
1304 First Procession of the Holy Blood
1350 Reconstruction in stone of the
      Belfry after the destruction of
      its wooden predecessor
1376-1420 Construction of the City Hall

The city gets her second wind   (1500-1578)

1506 The cloth merchant Jan Mouscron
      acquires Michelangelo's *Madonna
      with Child*
1528 Lancelot Blondeel designs the mantelpiece of the Liberty of Bruges
1548 Birth of the scientist Simon Stevin
1562 Marcus Gerards engraves the first
      printed town map of Bruges
1578 Bruges joins the rebellion against
      the Spanish king

An impoverished town in a pauperised Flanders (1584-1885)

1584 Bruges becomes reconciled with the Spanish king

1604 The Zwin is closed off

1713-1795 Austrian period

1717 Foundation of the Academy of Fine Arts, predecessor of the Groeninge Museum

1795-1814 French occupation

1799 Demolition of Saint Donatian's Cathedral and renovation of Burg

1815-1830 United Kingdom of the Netherlands

1830 Independence of Belgium; birth of the poet Guido Gezelle

1838 First railway station

The new city (1971-…)

1971 Amalgamation Law incorporates former suburbs

1985 King Baudouin opens new sea lock at Zeebrugge

2000 Historic city centre is given World Heritage status; Euro 2000 (European Football Championships)

2002 Cultural Capital of Europe

2008 *In Bruges* is released worldwide in cinemas

2010 The Procession of the Holy Blood is granted Intangible Cultural Heritage status by UNESCO

1600	1700	1800	1900	2000

Provincial town with revived ambitions (1885-1970)

1887 Unveiling of the statue of Jan Breydel & Pieter de Coninck (Markt)

1892 Publication of *Bruges la Morte* by Georges Rodenbach

1896 Start of the construction of the seaport

1897 Dutch becomes the official language; Dutch Yeast and Methylated Spirits Works

1902 First exhibition of the Flemish Primitives

1914-1918 The Great War; Zeebrugge becomes a German naval base

1940-1945 Historic city centre survives Second World War almost unscathed

1958 First Pageant of the Golden Tree

Brugge City Card
Endless bargains!

Would you like to explore Bruges and go easy on your wallet at the same time? Would you like to enjoy special offers whilst getting to know the city in all its aspects? With the Brugge City Card you will accumulate one discount after another and even visit countless attractions completely free of charge. This super bargain card is handy, inexpensive and offers a unique chance to save more than € 250.00!

HOW DOES IT WORK?

Choose the validity period yourself: 48hrs or 72hrs. In the chapters *Exploring Bruges, Getting Around in Bruges* and *Excursions from Bruges* onwards, you will find a detailed overview of all museums, places of interest and attractions in and around Bruges. If you see a 🔲 then the Brugge City Card lets you in for free. If you see a 🔲 , then you receive a hefty discount of at least 25% on the individual price. In addition, the free monthly magazine events@brugge handily lists all the events where the Brugge City Card offers you an extra discount.

The card will be automatically activated as soon as you use it for the first time. The card expires once the time-limit has been exceeded. You can visit each attraction only once. Bear in mind that most museums are closed on Mondays.

These are our special offers!

» Free entrance to 26 museums and places of interest in Bruges, including a hefty discount at the Historium Bruges and the museum shops to boot! Admire the world-famous paintings of the Flemish Primitives, gaze down onto the city from the top of the majestic Belfry and visit Choco-Story, the world's largest chocolate museum, or one of the other prestigious art collections.

» A free round trip on the canals (departures are only guaranteed in the period 1 March-15 November)! This is your chance to experience Bruges as never before and to explore its secret nooks and crannies and its romantic hotspots!

» At least 25% discount on not to be missed concerts, dance and theatre performances!

» At least 25% discount on your bike rental!

» At least 25% discount at your underground car park!

» At least 25% discount at various museums, places of interest and attractions in the vicinity of Bruges!

» Only € 6.00 for a three-day pass of De Lijn, valid on all buses and trams in the whole of Flanders!

WHAT WILL IT COST YOU?

	BRUGGE CITY CARD	BRUGGE CITY CARD -26
48h	€ 38,00	€ 35,00
72h	€ 43,00	€ 40,00

HOW TO PLACE AN ORDER?

Call in at the information offices ℹ️ at the Markt (Historium), at 't Zand (Concertgebouw) or at the Stationsplein (Station, railway station), or order your City Card at www.bruggecitycard.be.

Visit museums and places of interest

▦	Archeologiemuseum (Archaeological Museum)	€4,00
▦	Arentshuis	€4,00
▦	Basiliek van het Heilig Bloed (schatkamer)	
	(Museum of the Basilica of the Holy Blood)	€2,00
▦	Begijnenhuisje (Beguine's house)	€2,00
▦	Belfort (Belfry)	€8,00
▦	Brouwerij (Brewery) De Halve Maan / guided tour + tasting	€7,00
▦	Brugse Vrije (Liberty of Bruges)	€4,00
▦	Choco-Story (Chocolate Museum)	€7,00
▦	Diamantmuseum Brugge (Bruges Diamond Museum)	
	+ diamond cutting demonstration	€10,00
▦	Expo Picasso	€8,00
▦	Frietmuseum (Belgian Fries Museum)	€6,00
▦	Gentpoort	€4,00
▦	Gezellemuseum (Gezelle Museum)	€4,00
▦	Groeningemuseum (Groeninge Museum)	
	including visit to the Arentshuis	€8,00
▦	Gruuthusemuseum (Gruuthuse Museum)	€8,00
▦	Kantcentrum (Lace Centre)	€3,00
▦	Koeleweimolen (Koelewei Mill)	€3,00
▦	Lumina Domestica (Lamp Museum)	€6,00
▦	Museum-Gallery Xpo Salvador Dalí	€10,00
▦	Onze-Lieve-Vrouwekerk (Church of Our Lady)	€6,00
▦	Onze-Lieve-Vrouw-ter-Potterie (Our Lady of the Pottery)	€4,00
▦	Sint-Janshospitaal (Saint John's Hospital) + pharmacy	€8,00
▦	Sint-Janshuismolen (Sint-Janshuis Mill)	€3,00
▦	Sound Factory/Lantaarntoren	€6,00
▦	Stadhuis (City Hall) including Brugse Vrije (Liberty of Bruges)	€4,00
▦	Volkskundemuseum (Folklore Museum)	€4,00
▦	Historium Bruges	€ 11 > € 8,25
▦	+ discounts in the museum shops of the city museums	-25%
▦	+ discount in the museum shop of the Bruges Diamond Museum	-10%

Culture and events

▦	Concertgebouw	-30%
▦	Cultuurcentrum Brugge (Cultural Centre)	-30%
▦	Kunstencentrum De Werf (Art Centre)	-25%

Gentpoort

Museum of the Basilica of the Holy Blood

Saint John's Hospital

Liberty of Bruges

Museums around Bruges

▦	Canada-Poland War Museum (Adegem)	€ 5,00 > € 4,00
▦	Centrum Ronde van Vlaanderen (Tour of Flanders Centre, Oudenaarde)	€ 8,00 > € 6,00
▦	In Flanders Fields Museum (Ypres)	€ 8,00 > € 5,50
▦	Mu.ZEE (Ostend)	€ 5,00 > € 3,75
▦	Mu.ZEE Ensorhuis (Ensorhouse, Ostend)	€ 2,00 > € 1,50
▦	Mu.ZEE Permekemuseum (Permeke Museum, Jabbeke)	€ 3,00 > € 2,25
▦	Museum Torhouts Aardewerk (Torhout Pottery Museum, Torhout)	€ 1,50 > € 1,00
▦	Romeins Archeologisch Museum (Roman Archaeological Museum, Oudenburg)	€ 5,00 > € 3,00
▦	Sint-Janshospitaal (Saint John's Hospital, Damme)	€ 1,50 > € 1,00
▦	Uilenspiegelmuseum (Damme)	€ 2,50 > € 1,50
▦	Wijnendale Castle (Torhout)	€ 5,00 > € 3,00

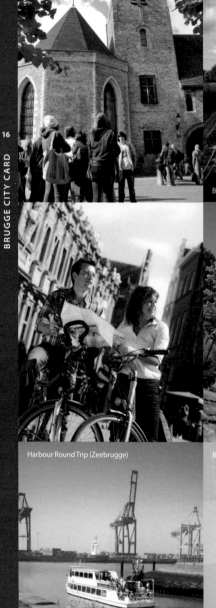

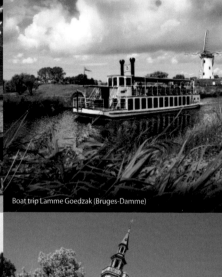

Boat trip Lamme Goedzak (Bruges-Damme)

Harbour Round Trip (Zeebrugge)

Boudewijn Seapark (Bruges)

Attractions around Bruges

▣	Boudewijn Seapark (Bruges)	€ 24,00 > € 15,00
▣	Seafront (Zeebrugge)	€ 12,50 > € 8,50

Sightseeing for next to nothing

▣	Bruges on foot (Jan., Feb., March, Nov., Dec.)	~~€ 9,00~~
▣	Bruges by boat	
	(departures are only guaranteed during the period 1/3-15/11)	~~€ 7,60~~
▣	City Tour Bruges (bus)	€ 16 > € 12
▣	Boat trip Lamme Goedzak Damme (return)	€ 10,00 > € 7,50
▣	Harbour Round Trip Zeebrugge	€ 10,00 > € 7,50
▣	Bruges Ballooning	€ 170,00 > € 127,50

Transport

▣	Parking Centrum-Zand/Centrum-Station/Pandreitje/Katelijne	- 25%
▣	3-day pass of De Lijn*	€ 6,00
▣	Electric Scooters (day rental)	class A: € 65 > € 48,75
		class B: € 75 > € 56,25

Bicycle rental points (day rental)

▣	Fietsen Popelier	€ 12,00 > € 9,00
▣	Fietsen 't Koffieboontje	€ 12,00 > € 9,00
▣	B-Bike Concertgebouw	€ 12,00 > € 9,00
▣	Bauhaus	€ 10,00 > € 6,00
▣	Bruges Bike Rental	bicycle: € 10,00 > € 7,50
		tandem: € 20,00 > € 15,00
▣	Fietspunt (railway station)	€ 12,00 > € 9,00

* Only available at the information offices [i] at the Markt (Historium), at 't Zand (Concertgebouw) or at the Stationsplein (Station, railway station).

Practical information

Bicycle rental points

Fietspunt Station
LOCATION > Hendrik Brugmansstraat 3
(Stationsplein, Railway station Square)
FEE > 1 hour: € 4.00; 4 hours: € 8.00; full day:
€ 12.00 (Brugge City Card: € 9.00)
OPENING TIMES > Monday-Friday 7.00 a.m.-
7.30 p.m.; weekends and public holidays
(1/4 > 15/11): € 9.00 a.m.-9.40 p.m.
CONTACT > tel. +32 (0)50 39 68 26

De Ketting
LOCATION > Gentpoortstraat 23
FEE > City bikes: € 6.00/day, electric bikes:
€ 20,00/day
OPENING TIMES > 7/7; 10.00 a.m.-6.30 p.m.
CONTACT > tel. +32 (0)50 34 41 96,
www.deketting.be

Eric Popelier
LOCATION > Mariastraat 26
FEE > 1 hour: € 4.00; 4 hours: € 8.00; full day:
€ 12.00 (Brugge City Card: € 9.00). Tandem 1 hour:
€ 10.00; 4 hours: € 17.00; full day: € 25.00 (Brugge
City Card: € 18.75); price reduction for students
OPENING TIMES > 7/7; 9.00 a.m.-7.00 p.m.
EXTRA > tandem bicycles
CONTACT > tel. +32 (0)50 34 32 62,
www.fietsenpopelier.be

Koffieboontje
LOCATION > Hallestraat 4
FEE > 1 hour: € 4.00; 4 hours: € 8.00; full day:
€ 12.00 (Brugge City Card: € 9.00); students:
€ 9.00. Tandem 1 hour: € 10.00; 4 hours:
€ 18.00; full day: € 25.00
OPENING TIMES > 7/7; 9.00 a.m.-10.00 p.m.
EXTRA > tandem bicycles, kiddie carriers (bike
trailers), children's seats, children's helmets,
elastic fasteners (for baggage), buggies for kids
and wheelchair, free cycle map
CONTACT > tel. +32 (0)50 33 80 27,
www.adventure-bike-renting.be

Bauhaus Bike Rental
LOCATION > Langestraat 145
FEE > 3 hours: € 6.00; full day: € 10.00
(Brugge City Card: € 6.00)

OPENING TIMES > 7/7; 9.00 a.m.-9.00 p.m.
(bikes must be returned by 9.00 p.m.)
CONTACT > tel. +32 (0)50 34 10 93,
www.bauhaus.be/bikes.html

Snuffel Backpacker Hostel
LOCATION > Ezelstraat 47-49
FEE > full day: € 8.00
OPENING TIMES > 7/7; 8.00 a.m.-8.00 p.m.
EXTRA > free cycle map
CONTACT > tel. +32 (0)50 33 31 33,
www.snuffel.be

B-Bike Concertgebouw
LOCATION > 't Zand
FEE > 1 hour: € 4.00; 4 hours: € 8.00; full day:
€ 12.00 (Brugge City Card: € 9.00)
OPENING TIMES > 1/4-15/10: daily: 10.00 a.m.-
12.00 a.m. and 1.00 p.m.-7.00 p.m. 16/10-31/3:
weekends only 10.00 a.m.-12.00 a.m. and
1.00 p.m.-7.00 p.m.
CONTACT > tel. +32 (0)479 97 12 80

Bruges Bike Rental
LOCATION > Niklaas Desparsstraat 17
FEE > 1 hour: € 3.50; 2 hours: € 5.00; 4 hours:
€ 7.00; full day: € 10.00 (Brugge City Card:
€ 7.50); students: € 8.00. Tandem 1 hour:
€ 8.00; 2 hours: € 12.00; 4 hours: € 15.00;
full day: € 20.00 (Brugge City Card: € 15.00)
OPENING TIMES > 7/7; 10.00 a.m.-10.00 p.m.

EXTRA > tandem bicycles, baskets, saddle-bags, baby/child's saddles and bike stretchers
CONTACT > tel. +32 (0)50 61 61 08, www.brugesbikerental.be

Church services

» **Basiliek van het Heilig Bloed (Basilica of the Holy Blood)**
daily (except Thursday) 11.00 a.m.
» **Begijnhofkerk (Beguinage)**
Monday-Saturday: 7.15 a.m., Sunday 9.30 a.m.
» **English Church**
(English language service, Anglican)
Saint Peter's Chapel, Keersstraat 1
Sunday 6.00 p.m.
» **Heilige Familiekerk (Holy Family)**
Saturday 5.30 p.m.
» **Heilige Magdalenakerk (Holy Magdalene)**
Sunday 11.30 a.m.
» **Jezuïetenhuis (Jesuits)**
Monday-Friday: 12.00 a.m., Saturday: 17.00 p.m., Sunday: 11.30 a.m.
» **Kapucijnenkerk (Capuchins)**
Monday-Friday 8.00 a.m., Saturday 6.00 p.m., Sunday 7.00 a.m. & 10.30 a.m.
» **Karmelietenkerk (Carmelites)**
Monday-Friday 7.00 a.m., Saturday: 6.00 p.m., Sunday: 10.00 a.m.
» **Onze-Lieve-Vrouwekerk (Church of Our Lady)**
Monday-Friday 9.00 a.m., Saturday 5.30 p.m., Sunday 11.00 a.m.
» **Onze-Lieve-Vrouw-ter-Potteriekerk (Our Lady of the Pottery)**
Monday-Friday: 6.45 a.m., Sunday: 7.00 a.m. & 9.30 a.m.
» **Onze-Lieve-Vrouw-van-Blindekenskapel (Our Lady of the Blind)**
Saturday 6.00 p.m.
» **Orthodoxe Kapel (Orthodox Church)**
Ezelstraat 85
Saturday 6.00 p.m., Sunday 9.00 a.m.
» **Sint-Gilliskerk (Saint Giles)**
Sunday 10.00 a.m.
» **Sint-Godelieveabdij (Saint Godelina's Abbey)**
Monday-Saturday: 8.25 a.m., Sunday: 9.30 a.m.
» **Sint-Jakobskerk (Saint Jacob)**
Saturday 6.30 p.m.
» **Sint-Salvatorskathedraal (Saint Saviour)**
Monday-Friday 6.00 p.m., Saturday 4.00 p.m., Sunday 10.30 a.m.

» **Sint-Walburgakerk (Saint Walburga)**
Sunday 7.00 p.m.
» **Verenigde Protestantse Kerk (United Protestant Church)**
't Keerske, Keersstraat 1
Sunday 10.00 a.m.
» **Vrije Evangelische Kerk (Free Evangelical Church)**
Naaldenstraat 18
Sunday 10.00 a.m.

Cinemas

» All films are shown in their original language.

08 Cinema Liberty
Kuipersstraat 23, www.cinema-liberty.be | Map: E7

09 Cinema Lumière
Sint-Jakobsstraat 36, www.lumiere.be | Map: D7

10 Kinepolis Brugge
Koning Albert I-laan 200, Sint-Michiels, www.kinepolis.com/brugge | Map: B14

Climate

Bruges enjoys a mild, maritime climate, with no great highs and lows. The summers are warm, without being hot. And the winters are cold, without being freezing. During spring and autumn the temperatures are also pleasant and there is moderate rainfall throughout the year, with the heaviest concentrations in autumn and winter. So remember to bring your umbrella!

Emergencies

▶ **European emergency number**
» tel. 112
This general number is used in all countries of the European Union to contact the emergency services: police, fire brigade or medical assistance. The number operates 24 hours a day, 7 days a week.

▶ **Medical help**
» **Doctors on duty**
7.00 p.m.-8.00 a.m. > tel. +32 (0)78 15 15 90
» **Pharmacists on duty**
tel. +32 (0)900 10 500

» **Dentists on duty**
tel. +32 (0)903 39 969

» **S.O.S. Emergency Service**
tel. 100

» **Hospitals**
A.Z. St.-Jan > tel. +32 (0)50 45 21 11
A.Z. St.-Lucas > tel. +32 (0)50 36 91 11
St.-Franciscus Xaveriuskliniek >
tel. +32 (0)50 47 04 70

» **Poisons Advice Centre**
tel. +32 (0)70 245 245

▶ **Police**

» **General telephone number**
tel. +32 (0)50 44 88 44

» **Emergency police assistance**   tel. 101

» **Working hours**
Monday-Friday: 8.00 a.m.-12.00 a.m. & 1.30 p.m.
-5.00p.m. (Tuesday: till 6.00 p.m.), Saturday:
8.00 a.m.-11.45 a.m. you can contact the servic-
es at Kartuizerinnenstraat 4 | city map: E9

» **After working hours**
There is a permanence at Hauwerstraat 3 (city
map: C10). These services, however, will move in
mid-2013 to Lodewijk Coiseaukaai 3 (city map: F1)

Formalities

» **Identity**
An identity card or valid passport is necessary.
Citizens of the European Union do not require
an entrance visa. If you arrive in Belgium from
outside the European Union, you must first
pass through customs. There are no border
controls once inside the European Union.

» **Health**
Citizens of the European Union can use their
own national health insurance card/docu-
ment to obtain free medical treatment in
Belgium. You can obtain this card from your
own national health service. Please note,
however, that every member of the family
must have his/her own card/document.

Getting there

» **By train**
» London – Bruges by Eurostar in 3.05 hours,
one transfer in Brussels (station Midi/Zuid).
» Also one transfer at Brussels (Midi/Zuid)
when coming from other European cities like

Amsterdam, Paris, Rotterdam, Cologne and
Luxembourg. Multiple direct connections
each day from Brussels, Ghent and Antwerp,
but also from other Belgian cities to Bruges.

» **By car / coach / ferry**
» Dover (UK) – Dunkirk (F) with DFDS Seaways |
Dunkirk (F) > Bruges (B) by car: 45 miles /
50 minutes.
» Dover (UK) – Calais (F) with DFDS Seaways
or P&O ferries | Calais (F) > Bruges by car:
72 miles / 80 minutes.
» Ramsgate (UK) – Ostend (B) with Tran-
seuropa Ferries| Oostende > Bruges by car:
15 miles / 25 minutes.
» Hull (UK) – Zeebrugge (B) with P&O ferries |
Zeebrugge > Bruges by car: 10 miles /
20 minutes.
» Rosyth (UK) – Zeebrugge (B) with DFDS Sea-
ways | Zeebrugge > Bruges by car: 10 miles /
20 minutes.

Please note! Maximum speed limit in the city
centre is 30 km/h.

» **By plane**
» **Via Brussels Airport**
Daily flights from 200 destinations in 66 coun-
tries. Easy access to Bruges by train (one
transfer in Brussels- Midi/Zuid).
» **Via Brussels-South-Charleroi-Airport**
Multiple flights a week with low-cost airlines

» How to get to Bruges?

Departure	via	km	mls	🚂 ⊙	🚢 ⊙	Make a reservation
Amsterdam	Antwerpen	253	157	3:56	-	www.b-rail.be
Köln	Brussel Midi/Zuid	313	194	2:47	-	www.bahn.de
London St.-Pancras	Brussel Midi/Zuid	-	-	3:21	-	www.eurostar.com
Lille	Kortrijk	75	47	1:20	-	www.b-rail.be
Paris	Brussel Midi/Zuid	296	184	2:37	-	www.thalys.com
Brussels Airport	Brussel-Noord	110	68	1:26	-	www.b-rail.be
Hull	Zeebrugge	-	-	-	1 night	www.poferries.com
Dover	Dunkerque	-	-	-	2:00	www.dfds.com
Ramsgate	Oostende	-	-	-	5:30	www.transeuropaferries.com
Dover	Calais	-	-	-	1:30	www.poferries.com
Dover	Calais	-	-	-	1:30	www.dfds.com

from several European cities. There is a regular train connection between Brussels-South airport and Brussels Midi/Zuid railway station. Frequent train connections between Brussels Midi and Bruges.

More information on www.bruges.be/transport

Good to know

With its wide shopping streets, inviting terraces, trendy eating houses and stylish hotels, Bruges is a paradise for shoppers. But don't let your shopping pleasure be ruined by pickpockets. Always keep your wallet/purse in a closed inside pocket, and not in an open handbag or rucksack. Remember – thieves like shopping too!

Bruges is a lively, fun-loving city, with great night-life. There are plenty of places where you can amuse yourself until the early hours of the morning. But please bear in mind the following regulations.

» It is forbidden to provide beer or wine (alcoholic drinks of more than 0.5 %) to people under the age of 16 years and strong drink (15% or more) to people under the age of 18 years.

» It is forbidden to consume alcohol on the street in the night-life district on Thursday, Friday and Saturday night.

Visiting Bruges means endless hours of fun, but please allow the visitors who come after you to enjoy their fun in a clean and tidy city: so always put your rubbish in a rubbish bin. Thank you.

Hours of opening

Most shops open their doors at 10.00 a.m. and close at 6.00 p.m. or 6.30 p.m from Monday to Saturday. Some shops are also open on Sunday afternoon. Cafés and restaurants have no (fixed) closing hour. Sometimes they will remain open until the early hours of the morning and sometimes they will close earlier: it all depends on the number of customers.

Info offices

There are three tourist information offices in Bruges: one in the Concertgebouw (Concert Hall), one in the recently opened Historium (Market Square) and one in the railway station.

» **Info office Markt (Historium)**
Markt 1
Daily: 10.00 a.m.-5.00 p.m.
Closed on Christmas Day and New Year's Day

» **Info office 't Zand**
(Concertgebouw, Concert Hall)
't Zand 34
Monday-Saturday: 10.00 a.m.-5.00 p.m.
Sunday and public holidays: 10.00 a.m.-2.00 p.m.
Closed on Christmas Day and New Year's Day

» **Info office Stationsplein**
(Station, railway station)
Stationsplein

Monday-Friday: 10.00 a.m.-5.00 p.m.
Saturday & Sunday: 10.00 a.m.-2.00 p.m.
Closed on Christmas Day and New Year's Day

Market days

» **Mondays**
8.00 a.m.-1.00 p.m. | Onder de Toren -
Lissewege | miscellaneous
» **Wednesdays**
8.00 a.m.-1.00 p.m. | Markt | food & flowers
» **Fridays**
8.00 a.m.-1.00 a.m. | Market Square -
Zeebrugge | miscellaneous
» **Saturdays**
8.00 a.m.-1.00 p.m. | 't Zand & Beursplein |
miscellaneous
» **Sundays**
8.00 a.m.-1.00 p.m. | Veemarkt, Sint-Michiels |
miscellaneous
» **Tuesdays to saturdays**
8.00 a.m.-1.00 p.m. | Vismarkt | fish
» **Saturdays, Sundays, public holidays
and bridge days in the period 15 March -
15 November + also on Fridays in the period
1 June - 30 September**
10.00 a.m.-6.00 p.m. | Dijver & Vismarkt |
antique, bric-a-brac and crafts

Money

Most of the banks in Bruges are open from 9.00
a.m. to 12.00 p.m. and from 2.00 p.m. to 4.30 p.m.
Many branch offices are also open on Saturday
morning, but on Sunday they are all closed.
There are cash points in the most important
shopping streets, on the Markt (Market
Square),'t Zand, Simon Stevinplein, Stationsplein (Railway station Square and on the Ka-
naaleiland (Canal Island, in the Bargeweg). You
can withdraw cash from these machines at any
time of the day or night, using your Visa, Euro-
card or Mastercard. Currency can be exchanged
in every bank or in an exchange office.
» **Goffin Change**
Steenstraat 2 | City map: E8
» **Pillen R.W.J.**
Rozenhoedkaai 2 | City map: F8

Parking

Bruges is a compact city. Most places of interest are within walking distance of your accommodation. In order to keep the historic
city centre attractive and accessible, above-
ground parking in the city centre is limited to
a maximum of 4 hours in the Blue Zone and
to 2 hours in the Pay&Display Zones. You
can easily park your car in one of the underground car parks. The most inexpensive and
largest car park is next to the railway station:
you pay € 3.50 a day, bus transfer with De Lijn
to and from the city centre for 4 passengers
included.
These buses leave every two minutes. The
Park and Ride areas are situated in walking
distance of the city centre. Here you can park
your car for free and for longer duration. The
city centre is a stone's throw away on foot or
by bus.

Parking Centrum-Zand

CAPACITY > 1400
OPENING TIMES > 24 hours a day,
7 days a week
RATES > day price: max. € 8.70/24-hour park-
ing | hourly rate: € 1.20; from the second hour
you pay per quarter

Parking Centrum-Station

CAPACITY > 1500
OPENING TIMES > 24 hours a day,
7 days a week
RATES > hourly rate: € 0.70
(maximum € 3.50/24hrs)

Post Offices

» **BPost Markt**
Markt 5 | City map: E8
» **BPost Beursplein**
Sint-Maartensbilk 14 | City map: B10

Public holidays

Belgium has quite a lot of public holidays.
On these holidays most companies, shops,
offices and public services are closed.
» 1 January (New Year's Day)
» Easter Sunday and Easter Monday
» 1 May (Labour Day)
» Ascension Day
» Whit Sunday and Whit Monday
» 11 July (Flemish regional holiday)
» 21 July (Belgian national holiday)
» 15 August (Ascension of the Blessed Virgin)

- » 1 November (All Saint's)
- » 11 November (Armistice Day)
- » 25 December (Christmas)
- » 26 December (Boxing Day)

Public transport
▶ LIJN Buses
You can use public transport during your stay. De Lijn connects the railway station and the centre by a bus every two minutes. From Bargeplein (city map F13), close to the spot where the tourist buses stop, there are also frequent services to the station and the city centre. All the city's bus stops are marked with a bus pictogram on the fold-out map at the back of this guide.

▶ Tickets
» **Advanced booking offices**
De Lijnwinkel, Stationsplein (railway station) Concertgebouw, 't Zand
Various city centre book shops, newspaper stands and department stores
» **Vending machines De Lijn**
De Lijnwinkel, Stationsplein (railway station) Busstop, 't Zand
» **Information** www.delijn.be

Smoking
In Belgium smoking is forbidden in pubs, cafés, restaurants and public buildings. Those unable to kick the habit will usually find an ashtray just outside (often under shelter), so that they can puff away to their heart's content in the open air.

Swimming Pools
» **11 Interbad**
INFO > Veltemweg 35, Sint-Kruis; tel. +32 (0)50 35 07 77, interbad@skynet.be; bus: nr. 11, Stop: Sint-Andreaslyceum

» **12 Jan Guilini**
INFO > Keizer Karelstraat 41, tel. +32 (0)50 31 35 54, sportdienst@brugge.be); bus: nr. 9, Stop: Visartpark

» **13 Olympia**
INFO > Doornstraat 110, Sint-Andries; tel. 050 39 02 00, olympiabad@west-vlaanderen.be, www.west-vlaanderen.be/olympiabad; bus: nr. 25, Stop: Jan Breydel

All information about opening times is available at the information office ℹ Markt (Historium), 't Zand (Concertgebouw) or Stationsplein (Station, railway station).

Travelling season
Although most visitors come to the city in the spring and summer months, Bruges has something to offer all year round. The misty months of autumn and winter are ideal for atmospheric strolls along the canals and the cobbled streets, before ending up in a cosy restaurant or cheerful pub. The 'cold' months are also perfect for undisturbed visits to the city's many museums and sites of interest, before again finishing up in one of those same restaurants or pubs! What's more, in January, February and March you can get great discounts on many accommodation outlets in Bruges.

Taxis
TAXI RANKS > Markt & Stationsplein

Telephoning
Now that nearly everyone has their own cell phone, there are very few public telephone boxes left in Bruges. If you want to phone someone in Bruges from abroad, you must first dial the country code (00)32, followed by the zone code 50, and then number of the person you want. To phone Bruges from inside Belgium, you dial 050 plus the number of the person.

Toilets
There are a number of public toilets in Bruges (see the fold-out plan at the back of the guide). Some are accessible for wheelchair users, others have baby-changing areas. You will also find free toilets in some of the larger department stores or at the station. When local people need the toilet, they often pop into a cafe or pub to order something small, so that they can use the facilities there.

Exploring Bruges

You might want to stroll, amble and saunter down the streets of
Bruges all day long or even for a whole weekend - nothing wrong
with that. However, why not try to see the city from a different perspective? During a walking or bicycle tour, a guide will show you
numerous secret places. Maybe you would prefer a boat trip on
the mysterious canals – an unforgettable experience! And a ride in
a horse-drawn carriage must surely be the perfect romantic out-
ing. Sport-lovers can even do a guided run around the city. Or perhaps you simply want to tour all the highlights as quickly and as
comfortably as possible? Then a minibus with expert commentary
is what you need. And what about a balloon ride or a daytrip on a
Vespa or an electric scooter? The choice is yours!

☐ 🚤 Bruges by Boat

A visit to Bruges isn't complete without a boat trip on its canals. Go aboard at any of the five landing stages (consult city map) for a half-hour trip that allows you to appreciate the most noteworthy delights of the city from a completely different angle. March- November: daily 10.00 a.m.-6.00 p.m.

FEE > € 7.60; children aged 4 to 11 (accompanied by an adult): € 3.40; children under 4: free; Brugge City Card (1/3 > 15/11): free

Bruges on Foot

Not exhausted from walking around yet? Are you still in the mood for a guided tour? Then hurry to 🛈 information office at 't Zand (Concertgebouw) and register for a two-hour fascinating guided walk. Languages: English, Dutch and French ☐ Jan./Feb./March/Nov./Dec.: Monday, Wednesday, Saturdag, Sunday

April/May/June/Sept./Oct.: during the weekends
July/August + Easter holidays (1/4-14/4) + second Ascension (10/5): daily
Start on Sundays and public holidays *: 10.30 a.m.
Other days at 2.30 p.m. (Apr-Oct) or at 4.00 p.m. (Nov-Mar)
*public holidays: Ascension of Our Lady (15/8), All Saints (1/11), Armistice Day (11/11) and Christmas (25/12)

FEE > € 9.00; children under 12: free; walks in Jan., Feb., March, Nov. and Dec. are free with Brugge City Card

TICKETS > Information office at 't Zand (Concertgebouw)] or www.tickets-brugge.be

Running around Bruges

Tourist Run Brugge – guided tours
Accompanied by a guide you run – at a gentle pace – through the streets and alleyways of Bruges. Because you either

run early in the morning (before the city wakes up) or early in the evening (after the hustle and bustle of the day has passed), you can admire Bruges in all its glory. The circuit is 9.5 km long. With the explanation that you receive along the way, you should allow 1 to 1.5 hours for completion. The start and finish are both on the Market Square, at the foot of the statues of Jan Breydel and Pieter de Coninck. On Saturdays and on the evenings before public holidays at 6.30 p.m.; on Sundays and public holidays at 8.00 a.m. Prior reservation is necessary. Special arrangements can be made for groups.

PRICE > € 15.00 (including drink, energy bar and map of the route, with tips)

INFORMATION > tel. +32 (0)473 88 37 17, www.touristrunbrugge.be

Bruges By Horse-drawn Carriage

The half-hour carriage ride along Bruges' historic winding streets trots off on Markt (at Burg on Wednesday morning). Halfway through the ride the carriage briefly stops at the Beguinage. The coachman gives expert commentary en route. 9.00 a.m.-6.00 p.m.; 9.00 a.m.-

10.00 p.m. in July and August.

FEE > € 39.00 per carriage; a carriage seats up to 5 people

INFO > www.bruges.be/tourism

Bruges by Hot Air Balloon

🎈 Bruges Ballooning

With Bruges Ballooning you can discover the city from a hot air balloon. A morning flight (champagne breakfast included) or an evening flight (champagne, snacks and beer included) lasts three hours, of which at least one is spent up in the air! On request only. Reservation for a balloon trip on the day itself is however possible until a few hours before departure.

FEE > € 170.00; children under 13: € 110.00; Brugge City Card: € 127.50

INFORMATION > tel. +32 (0)475 97 28 87 or www.bruges-ballooning.com

🚌 Bruges by bus

🚌 City Tour Brugge

The minibuses call at the different highlights of the city. They leave every hour from Markt for a fifty-minute trip. Headphones provide commentary in English, Dutch, French, German, Spanish, Italian and Japanese. The first bus leaves at 10.00 a.m. The last bus leaves at 4.00 p.m. in January and February, 5.00 p.m. in March, November and December, 6.00 p.m. in October, 7.00 p.m. in April, May and June, and 8.00 p.m. in July, August and September.

FEE > € 16.00; children aged 6 to 11: € 9.50; Brugge City Card: € 12.00

INFORMATION > tel. +32 (0) 50 35 50 24 (Monday-Friday 10.00 a.m.-12.00 a.m) or info@citytour.be, www.citytour.be

Bruges by bike

QuasiMundo Biketours Bruges

> 'Bruges By Bike': March-November, daily: 10.00 a.m.-12.30 p.m.

The narrow streets reveal the medieval character of the ancient port. The fascinating stories by the guide will catapult you back to a time when knights and counts ruled the town. It goes without saying that there is a stop along the way for a thirst-quenching Belgian beer.

> 'Border By Bike': March-November, daily: 1.00 p.m.-5.00 p.m. A tour through the flat countryside around Bruges, passing through medieval towns such as Damme, peaceful Flemish agrarian villages and

dead straight canals.

Meeting Point: at the statue of 'De Geliefden' (The Lovers) on Burg, ten minutes before departure of tour. English and Dutch spoken. Guides are also available in French, German and Spanish. Booking is recommended.

FEE > € 27.00; youngsters under 27: € 25.00; children under 9: free; € 16.00 if you bring your own bike. Tour includes guide, raincoat, water and refreshment in a local café.

INFORMATION > tel. +32 (0)50 33 07 75, www.quasimundo.com

The Pink Bear Bike Tours

A mere five minutes away from bustling Bruges lies one of the prettiest rural areas in Europe. You ride to historic Damme, the handsome medieval market town, once Bruges' outport. A guide will furthermore show you the most enchanting places of the Polders. It goes without saying that there is also a stop at a pleasant café for some Belgian Beers and/or Belgian waffles. On your return you follow the beautiful poplarplanted banks of a canal and discover some of Bruges' best-kept secrets. 10.25 a.m.-2.00 p.m. Meeting Point: Belfry. English is spoken, but the guides are also multilingual. In theory, there are tours every day. Only possible in January and February with prior reservation.

FEE > € 23.00; youngsters under 27: € 21.00; children under 9: free; € 16.00 if you bring your own bike.

INFORMATION > tel. +32 (0)50 61 66 86, www.pinkbear.freeservers.com

**The Green Bike Tour/
The Sun Bike Tour**

A guided trip to the polders, the flat countryside around Bruges. The tour pulls up at medieval Damme and other important sights along the way for a little extra commentary. From 10.00 a.m. to early afternoon from April to October. By appointment only during the low season. New in

2013 are the tandem rides. Meeting point:
[i] 't Zand (Concertgebouw). English, Dutch and French spoken. Booking recommended.

FEE > € 15.00; € 9.00 if you bring your own bike.

INFORMATION > tel. +32 (0)50 61 26 67, arlando@pandora.be

> Addresses of locations where you can hire bikes are given in the section Practical Info *on page 18*

Bruges by scooter

🛵 Electric Scooters

For people who prefer to explore Bruges in motorised style and in an ecologically responsible manner. Tuesday-Sunday 10.00 a.m.-12.00 p.m. and 2.00 p.m.-6.00 p.m.

PRICE (INCLUDING USE OF HELMET) >
For an A-class scooter/1 person: 2 hours: € 30.00; 4 hours: € 50.00. A-class scooter/2 persons: 4 hours: € 50.00; 8 hours: € 65.00 (there is a discount on the day price for holders of a Bruges City Card: € 48.75)
For a B-class scooter/2 persons: 4 hours:

€ 55.00; 8 hours: € 75.00 (there is a discount on the day price for holders of a Bruges City Card: € 56.25).

CONDITIONS > minimum age of driver = 23 years; for a B-class scooter: A3 or B category driving license; deposit of € 100.00 to be paid before departure.

OPEN > Tuesday-Sunday 10.00a.m.-12.00 p.m. and 2.00 p.m.–6.00 p.m.

INFORMATION > Gentpoortstraat 62, tel. +32 (0)51 57 00 02, www.electric-scooters.be

Vespa tours

Discover the Bruges' wet- and woodlands in style: book a guided tour with a snazzy Vespa scooter and traverse the green polders, authentic villages and breathtaking landscapes. A couple of surprises are provided en route. Half day and day tours. Booking essential. Meeting point: 't Zand. Dutch, French and English spoken.

FEE > half day tour: 1 person per Vespa: € 65.00; 2 persons per Vespa: € 80.00; day tour: 1 person per Vespa: € 100.00; 2 persons per Vespa: € 115.00; helmets and guide included.

CONDITIONS > minimum age of driver: 21 years, driving licence B, deposit of € 200.00 to be paid before departure. New for 2013: Cook & Ride a Vespa, a day-long programme with a fun mix of cooking and sightseeing.

INFORMATION > tel. +32 (0)497 64 86 48, bdpvespatours@gmail.com 00 www.vespatours-brugge.be

Award-winning restaurants

Bruges is called the epicentre of the world's gastronomy for good reason. The city places itself on the menu with an impressive list of first-class restaurants.

Michelin 2013   Source: Michelin Guide Belgium and Luxembourg 2013

» **De Karmeliet ★★★**   Chef Geert Van Hecke, Langestraat 19, 8000 Brugge, tel. +32 (0)50 33 82 59, www.dekarmeliet.be
» **Hertog Jan ★★★**   Chef Gert De Mangeleer, Torhoutse Steenweg 479, 8200 Sint-Michiels, tel. +32 (0)50 67 34 46, www.hertog-jan.com
» **Danny Horseele ★★**   Chef Danny Horseele, Stationsweg 45c, 8380 Dudzele, tel. +32 (0)50 32 10 32, www.restaurantdannyhorseele.be
» **De Jonkman ★★**   Chef Filip Claeys, Maalse Steenweg 438, 8310 Sint-Kruis, tel. +32 (0)50 36 07 67, www.dejonkman.be
» **A'Qi ★**   Chef Arnold Hanbuckers, Gistelse Steenweg 686, 8200 Sint-Andries, tel. +32 (0)50 30 05 99, www.restaurantaqui.be
» **Den Gouden Harynck ★**   Chef Philippe Serruys, Groeninge 25, 8000 Brugge, tel. +32 (0)50 33 76 37, www.goudenharynck.be
» **Auberge De Herborist ★**   Chef Alex Hanbuckers, De Watermolen 15, 8200 Sint-Andries, tel. +32 (0)50 38 76 00, www.aubergedeherborist.be
» **Sans Cravate ★**   Chef Henk Van Oudenhove, Langestraat 159, 8000 Brugge, tel. +32 (0)50 67 83 10, www.sanscravate.be

GaultMillau 2013   Source: GaultMillau, Belux 2013

» **Hertog Jan** (18,5/20)   Chef Gert De Mangeleer, Torhoutse Steenweg 479, 8200 Sint-Michiels, tel. +32 (0)50 67 34 46, www.hertog-jan.com
» **Danny Horseele** (18/20)   Chef Danny Horseele, Stationsweg 45c, 8380 Dudzele, tel. +32 (0)50 32 10 32, www.restaurantdannyhorseele.be
» **De Karmeliet** (18/20)   Chef Geert Van Hecke, Langestraat 19, 8000 Brugge, tel. +32 (0)50 33 82 59, www.dekarmeliet.be
» **De Jonkman** (18/20)   Chef Filip Claeys, Maalse Steenweg 438, 8310 Sint-Kruis, tel. +32 (0)50 36 07 67, www.dejonkman.be
» **A'Qi** (17/20)   Chef Arnold Hanbuckers, Gistelse Steenweg 686, 8200 Sint-Andries, tel. +32 (0)50 30 05 99, www.restaurantaqui.be

- » **Den Gouden Harynck** (17/20)   Chef Philippe Serruys, Groeninge 25, 8000 Brugge, tel. +32 (0)50 33 76 37, www.goudenharynck.be
- » **Auberge De Herborist** (16/20)   Chef Alex Hanbuckers, De Watermolen 15, 8200 Sint-Andries, tel. +32 (0)50 38 76 00, www.aubergedeherborist.be
- » **Sans Cravate** (16/20)   Chef Henk Van Oudenhove, Langestraat 159, 8000 Brugge, tel. +32 (0)50 67 83 10, www.sanscravate.be
- » **Zeno** (16/20)   Chef Reinout Reniere, Vlamingstraat 53, 8000 Brugge, tel. +32 (0)50 68 09 93, www.restaurantzeno.be
- » **'t Pandreitje** (15/20)   Chef Guy Van Neste, Pandreitje 6, 8000 Brugge, tel. +32 (0)50 33 11 90, www.pandreitje.be
- » **Patrick Devos** (15/20)   Chef Patrick Devos, Zilverstraat 41, 8000 Brugge, tel. +32 (0)50 33 55 66, www.patrickdevos.be
- » **Tanuki** (15/20)   Chef Ivan Verhelle, Oude Gentweg 1, 8000 Brugge, tel. +32 (0)50 34 75 12, www.tanuki.be
- » **Bistro Refter** (14/20)   Chef Frederiek Hoorne, Molenmeers 2, 8000 Brugge, tel. +32 (0)50 44 49 00, www.bistrorefter.be
- » **Bonte B** (14/20)   Chef Bernard Bonte, Dweersstraat 12, 8000 Brugge, tel. +32 (0)50 34 83 43, www.restaurantbonteb.be
- » **Goffin** (14/20)   Chef Timothy Goffin, Maalse Steenweg 2, 8310 Sint-Kruis, tel. +32 (0)50 68 77 88, www.timothygoffin.be
- » **Le Manoir Quatre Saisons** (14/20)   Chef Olivier Christiaens, Heilige-Geeststraat 1, 8000 Brugge, tel. +32 (0)50 34 30 01, www.castillion.be
- » **Rock Fort** (14/20)   Chef Hermes Vanliefde, Langestraat 15, 8000 Brugge, tel. +32 (0)50 33 41 13, www.rock-fort.be
- » **The Sixties** (14/20)   Hotel Ravestein, Chef Valentin Henneman, Molenmeers 11, 8000 Brugge, tel. +32 (0)50 47 69 47, www.restaurantsixties.be
- » **'t Stil Ende** (14/20)   Chef Frank Dehens, Scheepsdalelaan 12, 8000 Brugge, tel. +32 (0)50 33 92 03, www.stilende.be
- » **Weinebrugge** (14/20)   Chef Benny De Bruyn, Leikendreef 1, 8200 Sint-Michiels, tel. +32 (0)50 38 44 40, www.weinebrugge.be
- » **Burg 9** (13/20)   Chef Kristof de Kroon, Burg 9, 8000 Brugge, tel. +32 (0)50 33 35 99, www.burg9.be
- » **De Visscherie** (13/20)   Chef Björn Verriest, Vismarkt 8, 8000 Brugge, tel. +32 (0)50 33 02 12, www.visscherie.be
- » **Den Dyver** (13/20)   Chef Achim Vandenbussche, Dijver 5, 8000 Brugge, tel. +32 (0)50 33 60 69, www.dyver.be
- » **Kardinaalshof** (13/20)   Chef Stefan Dekerf, Sint-Salvatorskerkhof 14, 8000 Brugge, tel. +32 (0)50 34 16 91, www.kardinaalshof.be
- » **La Tâche** (13/20)   Chef Olivier Monbailliu, Blankenbergse Steenweg 1, 8000 Sint-Pieters, tel. +32 (0)50 68 02 52, www.latache.be

» **Lieven** (13/20)   Chef Lieven Vynck, Philipstockstraat 45, 8000 Brugge,
tel. +32 (0)50 68 09 75, www.etenbijlieven.be

» **Tête Pressée** (13/20)   Chef Pieter Lonneville, Koningin Astridlaan 100,
8200 Sint-Michiels, tel. +32 (0)470 21 26 27, www.tetepressee.be

» **'t Zwaantje** (13/20)   Chef Geert Vanhee, Gentpoortvest 70, 8000 Brugge,
tel. +32 (0)473 71 25 80, www.hetzwaantje.be

» **Channel 16** (👍)   Werfkaai 16, 8380 Zeebrugge, tel. +32 (0)50 60 16 16, www.ch16.be

» **De Florentijnen** (👍)   Academiestraat 1, 8000 Brugge, tel. +32 (0)50 67 75 33,
www.deflorentijnen.be

» **De Mangerie** (👍)   Oude Burg 20, 8000 Brugge, tel. +32 (0)50 33 93 36,
www.mangerie.com

» **Duc de Bourgogne** (👍)   Huidenvettersplein 12, 8000 Brugge,
tel. +32 (0)50 33 20 38, www.ducdebourgogne.be

» **Huyze Die Maene** (👍)   Markt 17, 8000 Brugge, tel. +32 (0)50 33 39 59,
www.huyzediemaene.be

» **'t Jong Gerecht** (👍)   Langestraat 119, 8000 Brugge, tel. +32 (0)50 31 32 32,
www.tjonggerecht.be

» **Kwizien Divien** (👍)   Hallestraat 4, 8000 Brugge, tel. +32 (0)50 34 71 29,
www.kwiziendivien.be

» **Parkrestaurant** (👍)   Minderbroedersstraat 1, 8000 Brugge, tel. +32 (0)497 80 18 72

Bib Gourmand 2013   Source: Bib Gourmand Benelux 2013

» **Assiette Blanche**   Chef Stefaan Timmerman, Philipstockstraat 23-25,
8000 Brugge, tel. +32 (0)50 34 00 94, www.assietteblanche.be

» **'t Apertje**   Chef Leo Callewaert, Damse Vaart-Zuid 223, 8310 Sint-Kruis,
tel. +32 (0)50 35 00 12, www.apertje.be

» **Bistro Refter**   Chef Frederiek Hoorne, Molenmeers 2, 8000 Brugge,
tel. +32 (0)50 44 49 00, www.bistrorefter.be

» **Bistro Kok au Vin**   Chef Jürgen Aerts, Ezelstraat 21, 8000 Brugge,
tel. +32 (0)50 33 95 21, www.kok-au-vin.be

» **Channel 16**   Chef Christian Van den Ouden, Werfkaai 16, 8380 Zeebrugge,
tel. +32 (0)50 60 16 16, www.ch16.be

» **Kurt's Pan**   Chef Kurt Van Daele, Sint-Jakobsstraat 58, 8000 Brugge,
tel. +32 (0)50 34 12 24, www.kurtspan.be

» **Tête Pressée**   Chef Pieter Lonneville, Koningin Astridlaan 100, 8200 Sint-Michiels,
tel. +32 (0)470 21 26 27, www.tetepressee.be

» **Restaurant Pergola**   Chef Nick Coppens, Meestraat 7, 8000 Brugge,
tel. +32 (0)50 44 76 50, www.pergolakaffee.be

Overnight stays in Bruges

Whether you opt for a classy four-star hotel, a charming B&B, a cheap-and-cheerful youth hostel or an authentic holiday home, one thing is certain: in Bruges there is always plenty of choice and you will always spend the night in style. There is something for everyone, no matter what your taste or budget is.

On the reverse side of the handy city plan – which you can remove from the back of this guide – you will find a list of licensed accommodation options, grouped by type. There are also useful directions for how to get to each licenced accommodation address – not only for people travelling by car, but also for users of public transport.

Accommodation reservations can be made online via www.bruges.be/tourism or directly with the outlet of your choice.

Souvenirs from Bruges

There is nothing more pitiful than returning home with a trivial souvenir that is immediately exiled to a cupboard – Bruges offers a solution. The World Heritage City impresses with a selection of authentic gadgets, novelties and other objects that you would dearly love to keep yourself. From unique lacework and glittering diamonds to foamy local beers and irresistibly delicious chocolate. Too good and too tempting to resist!

Because Bruges is easily accessible and because the main shopping streets are close to each other, a 'day at the shops' in the city's old historic centre is a pleasant and carefree experience. As well as the better-known chain stores, there is a wide range of smaller shops and boutiques. And for those who are prepared to step off the beaten track, there are always exciting discoveries to be made.

The most important shopping streets run from the Markt (Market Square) to the old city gates (the shopping area is coloured in yellow on the street plan). Hidden away between Noordzandstraat and Zuidzandstraat there is a small but interesting shopping centre: Zilverpand. Each neighbourhood has its own character. In the main shopping streets you will find the famous brands and names, while (for

example) the Langestraat is full of second-hand stores and interesting shops.

Lace

You don't fancy a boring, run-of-the-mill souvenir? Why not purchase some unique Bruges lace? A fine piece of fancywork with an incontestable reputation. Bruges and its lace have been inextricably bound up with one another since time immemorial. Thousands of female hands have brought Bruges lace its

deserved worldwide fame, and it also provided countless girls and women with a welcome addition to their income. Once half of the female population of Bruges was making bobbin lace. Today you can still see lacemakers at work here and there. It is such fun to try and follow their dexterity with their fingers. Or do you prefer an attempt at bobbin lacing yourself? At the Lace Centre experienced lacemakers will teach you the tricks of the trade. See page 84 for all practical information.

Beer

Let's not beat about the bush. A Brugean enjoys a pint of beer now and then, especially if the beer has been brewed in his own city. So it is logical that Bruges boasts no fewer than three local beers: 'Straffe Hendrik' and 'Brugse Zot', brewed by the De Halve Maan Brewery, and 'Bourgogne des Flandres', brewed by the brewery of

the same name. You won't find many beers like this. In short, they are internationally acclaimed success stories that taste of more, beers so full of character that you will definitely want to take them home with you in order to share them with the rest of the world. After all, it would be a shame to let only the citizens of Bruges smack their lips, wouldn't it? Convinced? Then return to the annual Bruges Beer Festival and discover even more hidden treasures! You can read more about the De Halve Maan and Bourgogne des Flandres breweries on page 77-78.

Diamonds

In the 14th century Bruges was already the centre of a thriving diamond industry. Diamonds were expertly cut here. This is really no surprise, because diamond cutting on a revolving disc was invented by the local goldsmith Lodewijk van Berquem in 1476. A year later the emperor

Maximilian of Austria offered Mary of Burgundy the very first diamond engagement ring in history. It is obvious the Dukes of Burgundy valued beauty very much. At the Diamond lab of the Bruges Diamond Museum you will be able to find some sparkling inspiration, and you will also learn how to assess all this brilliance. You will then be able to use your expert eye at the museum shop or the countless jeweller's in town before you seize your opportunity. Fancy something less expensive? Then surprise your loved one with a small rough or cut diamond from the Bruges Diamond Museum. See page 79 for detailed information.

Chocolate

A serious chocolate guild, the 'Brugsch Swaentje' (Bruges' Swan): the city's own delicious chocolate, a fascinating chocolate museum and even a scrumptious chocolate walk. What an abundance of quality guarantees, wouldn't you say? It only stands to reason that Bruges calls itself the chocolate capital of the world. In other words, if you don't succumb to a piece of chocolate here, you will never do so. Almost the entire city is covered in the sweet smell of this delicacy, as around every corner a chocolate temptation is lurking. Bruges counts more than fifty excellent chocolate shops, providing the visitor with whatever they're looking for, from exquisite old-fashioned solidity and delectable trinkets for own use to ingenious molecular chocolate hocus-pocus cooked up by Michelin starred chefs. You can discover more about chocolate on page 79.

Walking
in Bruges

» START	![i] 't Zand (Concertgebouw)
» DISTANCE	3 km
» FINISH	Saint John's Hospital

Walk 1

Bruges, proud World Heritage City

Bruges may be, quite rightly, very proud of her World Heritage status, but the city is happily embracing the future too! This walk takes you along world-famous panoramic views, sky-high monuments and centuries-old squares invigorated by contemporary constructions. One foot planted in the Middle Ages, the other one firmly planted in the present. This walk is an absolute must for first-time visitors who would like to explore the very heart of the city straight away. Keep your camera at the ready!

Oude Zak

Sint-Jansstraat

Naaldenstr.

Kuipersstraat

J. van Ooststr.

Kraan-plein

St.-Jans-plein

Ieperstr.

Wapenmakersstraat

St.-Walburgastraat

Ridder

Twijnstraat

22 Sint-Jakobs-plein

Leeuwstr.

St.-Jakobsstraat

Geerwijnstraat

Palmstr.

Niklaas Desparsstr.

Vlamingstraat

Cordoeaniersstr.

Keersstr.

Middel-burgstr.

Mallebergplaats

Hoogstraat

Hof Sebrechts

Geldmuntstraat

Eiermarkt

Ghisebrecht-straat

Philipstockstraat

Burgstr.

33 Muntplein
Muntpoort

St.-Amandsstr.

MARKT

Breidelstraat

BURG

Steenhouwersd.

Vismarkt

J. Suveebraam

Spikkelboorstr.

Prinsenhof

Korte Zilverstr.

Kleine St.-Amandsstr.

40

Huiden-vettersplein

13

Pandreitje

Geerolfstr.

Ontvangersstraat

Steenstraat

St.-Niklaasstr.

Hallestraat

Wollestraat

Kartuizerinnenstr.

Rozenhoedkaai

Eekhoutstr.

Gevang

Speelmansrei

Haanstraat

Wulfhagestraat

Giststraat

Kemelstr.

Oude Zakstr.

Dijver

Eekhoutpoort

't Pand

Willemstr.

Atoisstr.

Noordzandstraat

Zilverpand

Zilverstr.

Simon Stevinplein

St.-Salvators-kerkhof

Oude Burg

Nieuwstr.

Grauwwerkersstr.

Groeninge

Zuidzandstr.

23 St.-Salvatorskerkhof

H.-Geeststr.

Pipersstr.

Guido Gezelle-plein

Hof Arents

Lendestr.

Oranje-boomstr.

Kleine H.-Geeststr.

Mariastraat

O.L.V.-kerkhof-Zuid

Groeninge

Korte Vulderstr.

START

Goezeputstraat

OUD SINT-JAN
Congrescentrum

FINISH

Kastanjeboomstraat

Nieuwe Gen

St.-Jan in de Meers

Bakkersstr.

Koolbrandersstr.

St.-Obrechtsstr.

Stoofstraat

Walstraat

Driekroezenstr.

Zonnekemeers

Weversstr.

Walplein

Winnaardstraat

Oude Gentv

Visspaanstraat

Koning Albert I-laan

Koning Albertpark

Westmeers

Oostmeers

Garsoenstr.

BEGIJNHOF

Begijnhof

Wijngaard-plein

Noordstr.

Katelijnestraat

Suikerbergstraat

Unesco-rotonde

Eiland

Oostmeers

Prof. Dr. J. Sebrechtsstraat

Minnewater

Arsenaalstraat

Colettijnenstraat

Buiten Begijnenvest

Begijnenvest

Minnewaterpark

Minnewater

Colettijnen-hof

Katelijnevest

Kateljnestraat

Bargeweg

From 't Zand
to Simon Stevinplein

This walk starts at the Tourist Information office **i** 't Zand (Concertgebouw). 't Zand is dominated by the concert hall **14**, Bruges' new modern attraction. A clear-cut proof that this World Heritage city isn't afraid of the future. On the very top floor of this modern cube-shaped building you can find the Sound Factory; which is housed in the so-called Lantaarntoren (Lantern Tower) **39**. Don't forget to drop in at **i** 't Zand (Concertgebouw) on the ground floor: here you will find all the necessary tourist information as well as expert advice on all cultural events.

Leave **i** 't Zand (Concertgebouw) behind you, walk along the square and turn into Zuidzandstraat, the first street on the right. Saint Saviour's Cathedral **23** looms up ahead on your right after three hundred metres. Bruges' oldest parish church is located on its original street level, i.e. lower than the

TIP

Why not call in at the Sound Factory and let those Bruges bells ring! And because the Sound Factory is located in the Lantern Tower at the very top of the Concert Hall, you can enjoy a superb panorama over the city while the bells play your very own carillon composition.

present Zuidzandstraat. The street level gradually rose throughout the Middle Ages as people simply threw their refuse out onto the street where it was then flattened by passing carts and coaches. Inside Saint Saviour's, the church tower's wooden rafters can be lit. The cathedral treasury displays a.o. interesting copper memorial plaques, fine examples of gold and silver and paintings by Dieric Bouts, Hugo van der Goes and Pieter Pourbus.

Continue past the cathedral and walk down Sint-Salvatorskerkhof immediately on the right. Turn left into Sint-Sal-

vatorskoorstraat. Simon Stevinplein opens up at the end of this street. This attractive square, lined with cosy restaurant terraces, is named after Simon Stevin, a well-known Flemish-Dutch scientist. His gracious statue naturally takes centre stage.

Markt and Burg

Continue down Oude Burg, a street in the right-hand corner of the square. Before long you will see the Cloth Halls on your left. These belong to the Belfry **04**. You're allowed to cross the halls' imposing inner court between 8.00 a.m. and 6.00 p.m. during the week, and between 9.00 a.m. to 6.00 p.m. at weekends. The Markt is at the other end of the yard. If the gate is closed, turn back and walk down Hallestraat, which runs parallel to the Halls. Walk II (page 54) comments extensively on Markt.

Return to the Belfry **04** and walk down Breidelstraat, a traffic-free alley on the corner. Continue to Burg. Along the way on your right you will notice De Garre, a narrow alley. This may be the narrowest street in Bruges (try walking side by side here!), it nevertheless boasts a fair number of cosy cafés. Burg is the most majestic square in the city, so take your time to admire its grandeur. The main character in this medieval story is the City Hall **40** **09** (1376-1420), one of the oldest city halls in the Netherlands and a Gothic example for all its brothers and sisters that were built later, from Leuven to Oudenaarde and Brussels. Having admired its exterior, enter the impressive Gothic Hall and gaze in admiration at the polychrome floating ribs of the vaulted ceiling. Hiding on the right-hand side of this Gothic monument is the Basilica of the Holy Blood **01** , a mystical double chapel, below which sits the Roman-

BURG: AN ARCHITECTURAL SYNOPSIS

Art lovers have already noticed that Burg projects a wonderful cross-section of stunning architectural styles. It is, indeed, a summing-up in one place of all the styles that have caught our imagination throughout the various centuries. From Romanesque (Saint Basil's Church) and Gothic (City Hall) by way of Renaissance (Civil Registry) and Baroque (Deanery) to Classicism (Mansion of the Liberty of Bruges). There's no need to go and dash all around Bruges to see it all!

01

esque Church of Saint Basil (1139 1149).
One floor up is a basilica in Gothic revival style where the reliquary of the Holy
Blood has been kept since time immemorial. Each year on Ascension Day, the
reliquary is carried along in the Procession of the Holy Blood, a much-loved
event that has been warming the hearts
of the entire population from as early as
1304. Facing the basilica is the gleaming
Renaissance façade of the erstwhile Civil Registry **03** (1534-1537), which now
houses the City Archive **08** adjacent to
the Liberty of Bruges **12**. Its showpiece
is a splendid oak mantelpiece with an
alabaster frieze (1529). Adjoining is the
former mansion of the Liberty of Bruges
(1722-1727). It is from here that the country around Bruges was administered. Af-

ter 1795 a court of justice was installed.
It has been the city's administrative centre since 1988. Once upon a time Saint
Donatian's Cathedral graced the spot
directly in front of the City Hall. The
church was destroyed in 1799. Adjacent
to it is the Deanery (1655- 1666) **17**, of
the cathedral.

Fishy stories

Proceed to Blinde-Ezelstraat, the little
street to the left of the City Hall. Don't
forget to look back at the lovely arch
between City Hall and Old Civil Registry **03**. Do you see Solomon? Left of
him is the statue of Prosperity, to the
right the statue of Peace.
According to legend, Blinde-Ezelstraat
(Blind Donkey Street) owes its name to…
a blind donkey. The house in the left-
hand corner hugging the Canal used to
house a mill driven by a donkey. In order
to preserve the poor animal from the de-
pressing thought that the only thing it
had to do was turn endless rounds, a

TIP

Take a breather on a bench on the Burg
and enjoy the majestic splendour of
this square in all its glory.

blindfold was put on the donkey. A new street name was born. Look left on the bridge: Meebrug is said to be the oldest bridge in Bruges.

The Vismarkt  **opens up immediately past the bridge.**

At first, fish was sold on one of the Markt's corners, but as the townspeople complained about the stench, the fishmongers were forced to move and sell their wares here. In the covered arcade (1821), specially erected for the purpose of selling fish, fresh seafish was sold, a delicacy that only the rich could afford. Today you can still buy your fresh saltwater fish here every morning from Tuesday to Saturday.

Retrace your steps and turn left in front of the bridge towards Huidenvettersplein. Whereas the Vismarkt served the rich, Huidenvettersplein (Tanners Square) served the poor. No sea fish on the menu here, but affordable freshwater fish. The post in the middle of the square used to have a twin brother: in between the two posts hung the scales that the fish were weighed on. The large, striking building dominating the square used to be the guildhall of the tanners. Here they turned cow hides into leather. As this was a rather smelly job, it is no coincidence that the tanners' guildhall adjoined the fish markets. Look out for the statuette adorning the corner of the hall. It's no surprise that the little fellow raises his nose.

Continue to Rozenhoedkaai. Keep right. Rozenhoedkaai is the most photographed spot in Bruges, so get out your camera! So, take out your camera! This used to be the salt port. In the Middle Ages salt was as expensive as gold: it served to preserve food and to season dishes. A word like *salaris* (Dutch), *salaire* (French), salary still harks back to medieval times. The word derives from sal, which is Latin for salt. Roman soldiers' wages were paid in salt!

From Groeninge to the Bonifacius Bridge

Continue along Dijver.

Many centuries ago all manner of druids gathered on this holy spot to give praise to their gods and spirits. Along this atmospheric stretch of water, you will first find the College of Europe (numbers 9 to 11) **03**, an international postgraduate institution that focuses on European affairs, and then the Groeninge Museum (number 12) **23**, Bruges' most renowned museum. On display are world-famous masterpieces by Jan van Eyck, Hans Memling, Hugo van der Goes, Gerard David and many other Flemish Primitives. The museum also has a valuable collection of Flemish expressionists, neoclassical top notch paintings from the 18th and 19th centuries and post-war modern art. Overall, the museum shows a complete overview of Belgian and southern Dutch (Flemish) painting from the 15th to the 20th century. The museum entrance is reached through a few picturesque courtyard gardens. Would you like to find out more about the Flemish Primitives? Then leaf through to the interview on page 109 with Till-Holger Borchert, the Groeninge Museum's chief curator.

ALMSHOUSES, THE QUICKEST WAY TO HEAVEN

These 14th-century dwellings were charitable institutions, sometimes set up by the guilds to lodge their elderly members, sometimes set up by widows or well-to-do burghers who wanted to ensure their place in heaven. For that purpose, each set of almshouses had its own chapel where the occupants of the almshouses would be expected to send their prayers of thanks up to heaven. Practically all of the almshouses have been carefully restored and modernised and offer cosy living to today's elderly, whilst their small yet picturesque gardens and whitewashed façades offer welcoming peace and quiet to the present-day visitor. Feel free to enter these premises, but don't forget to respect their perfect tranquillity.

(On the map the Almshouses are indicated by 🏠 *)*

Continue along Dijver. The entrance gate to the Gruuthuse Museum **24** is on your left just beyond the little bridge. You learn more about Gruuthuse on page 52 (Walk II).

Continue to Guido Gezelleplein, then turn left in front of the Church of Our Lady **15** and follow the narrow footpath to the picturesque Bonifacius Bridge. The crosses that you see all over the place don't belong to graves at all - they are crosses taken down from church steeples during the First World War to disorientate the enemy spies. The crosses have never been put up again. Close

to the Bonifacius Bridge is Bruges' smallest Gothic window. Look up! It was through this window that the lords and ladies of Gruuthuse were able to peer down onto their private jetty. Across the bridge is the charming city garden 'Arentshof' of Arentshuis **02**, an elegant 18th-century abode. The top floor houses work by the versatile British artist Frank Brangwyn. The ground floor is reserved for temporary exhibitions. Rik Poot's remarkable sculpture group in the garden represents the Apocalypse: famine, death, revolution and the plague. A theme that appealed to the painter Hans Memling as well. Go through the garden gate to reach the Groeninge Museum **23**, where more work by Memling is displayed.

On to the Beguinage!

Leave the garden once more through the narrow garden gate and turn left into 'Groeninge,' a winding street. Turn right again at the intersection with Nieuwe Gentweg. Notice the Saint Jo-

---

TIP

If you visit the Gruuthuse Museum **24**, make sure you check out the small, red velvet chapel – a kind of religious *business seat* – that looks out over the altar of the Church of Our Lady (Onze-Lieve-Vrouwekerk).

seph Almshouses (17th century) and the De Meulenaere Almshouses (1613). Continue down the street.

On the left-hand corner of Oude Gentweg and Katelijnestraat is the Diamond Museum **18**, Bruges' most glittering museum and the place to be for all lovers of bling. It goes without saying that an inspiring diamond museum simply couldn't be absent in the most romantic city of the western hemisphere!

Turn left into Katelijnestraat, then immediately right into Wijngaardstraat. Cross Wijngaardplein – a stopping place for coachmen. A little further on turn right onto the bridge beside the Sashuis (lockhouse) to enter the Beguinage. The bridge offers a fine view of the Minnewater.

The Minnewater used to be the landing stage of the barges or track boats which provided a regular connection between Bruges and Ghent. Today it is one of Bruges' most romantic beauty spots. Equally atmospheric, yet of a totally different nature, is the Beguinage. Although the 'Princely Beguinage Ten Wijngaarde' **02** **02**, founded in 1245, is no longer occupied by beguines, but by nuns of the Order of Saint Benedict, you can still form an excellent picture of what daily life looked like in the 17th century at the Beguine's house **03**. The imposing courtyard garden, the whitewashed house fronts and blessed peace create an atmosphere all of its own. The entrance gate closes each day at 6.30 p.m. without fail. You have been warned!

Walk around the Beguinage and leave through the main gate. Turn left after the bridge and left again to reach Walplein.

De Halve Maan **11**, a brewery estab-

lished as early as 1546, is at number 26. This is Bruges' last active city brewery. Their speciality is 'Brugse Zot' (Bruges' Fool), a spirited top-fermented beer made from malt, hop and special yeast. The name of the beer refers to the nickname of the Bruges townspeople, a name allegedly conferred upon them by Maximilian of Austria. In order to welcome the duke, the citizens paraded past him in a lavish procession of brightly-coloured merrymakers and fools. When a short time later they asked their ruler to finance a new 'zothuis' or madhouse, his answer was as short as it was forceful: 'The only people I have seen here are fools. Bruges is one big madhouse. Close the gates!'

A splendid finish at Saint John's Hospital

Turn left into Zonnekemeers. Once across the water, turn right to enter the area of Old St. John via the car park. The former Hospital of Saint John (13th-14th century) **35** has a proud eight century-long history. The oldest documents even date back to the 12th century! Here nuns and monks took good care of pilgrims, travellers and the sick. And people sometimes chose to die here. Hans Memling once was a patient here too. According to a much later legend, he rewarded his benefactors with no fewer than six masterpieces.

Turn the corner, enter the building and weave your way through the medieval wards, the incorporated church, the Diksmuide attic and the old dormitory. Don't forget to pay a visit to the adjoining 17th-century pharmacy. The herb garden grows all the ingredients for gruut (gruit): lady's mantle, bog myrtle and bay laurel. On the picturesque square that leads to this garden is 'The Arteries of the Convent', a work by the contemporary Italian artist Giuseppe Penone. How history feeds the present. The World Heritage city of Bruges couldn't possibly find a better representation of her intentions. In Walk II – on page 52 – the meaning of *gruut* is explained.

» START	Guido Gezelleplein, Church of Our Lady
» DISTANCE	2,5 km
» FINISH	Prinsenhof

Walk 2

Bruges: B of Burgundian

When, during Bruges' Golden Age Philip the Bold, Duke of Burgundy, married Margaret of Dampierre, the daughter of the last Count of Flanders, the county of Flanders suddenly found itself belonging to Burgundy. As the Burgundian court liked to stay in Bruges, the port city became a magnet for noblemen, merchants and artists. They naturally all wanted to get their share of the city's wealth. Today the Burgundian influence is still strongly felt throughout Bruges. Let's discover a northern city with a southern character.

Hugo Losschaertstr.
Schuttersstr.
Kalkovenstr.
Achiel Van Ackerplein
Sterstraat
Sint-Gilliskoorstr.
Lange Raamstraat
Korte Raamstr.
Kleine Hoedenmakersstr.
Gistelhof
Schrijversstraat
Hoedenmakersstraat
West-Gistelhof
Oost-Gistelhof
Schottinnenstr.
Gouden-Handstraat
Torenbrug
Jan Boninstraat
Sint-Jorisstraat
Jan Miraelstr.
Augustijnenrei
Kortewinkel
Spaanse Loskaai
Spanjaardstraat
Oosterlingenplein
Gouden-Handrei
Krom Genthof
Korte Ble
Poitevinstraat
Pottenmakersstraat
P. Pourbusstr.
Vlamingstraat
Kipstraat
Rode-Haanstr.
Woensdagmarkt
Spiegelrei
Spinolarei
Genthof
Grauwwerkersstr.
Academiestraat
Jan van Eyckplein
Biskajersplein
Koningstr.
St.-Maartensplein
Zakske
Boterhuis
Adriaan Willaertstr.
Braambergstr.
Boudewijn-Ostenstr.
Sint-Janstraat
Engelstraat
Korte Ridderstr.
Oude Zak
Sint-Jakobsplein
Naaldenstr.
Kuiperstraat
J. van Ooststr.
Wijnzakstraat
Kraanrei
St.-Jansplein
Ieperstr.
Wapenmakersstr.
St.-Walburgastraat
Riddersstr.
Twijnstr.
Leeuwstr.
Hof Sebrechts
Geerwijnstraat
Palmstr.
St.-Jakobsstraat
Niklaas Desparsstr.
Kraanplein
Cordoeaniersstr.
Kaersstr.
Middel-burgstr.
Kelkstraat
Kl. Hem berges
Moerstraat
Muntplein
Muntpoort
Eiermarkt
Geernaart straat
Philipstockstraat
Burgstr.
Mallebergplaats
Hoogstraat
Meestraat
Her
Prinsenhof
FINISH
Ontvangersstraat
Geldmuntstr.
St.-Amandsstr.
Kleine St.-Amandsstr.
MARKT
Breidelstraat
BURG
Steenhouwersdijk
Vismarkt
J. Suvekerstr.
Braambergstr.
Helmstraat
Korte Zilverstr.
Hallestraat
De Garre
Blinde Ezelstr.
Huidenvettersplein
Rozenhoedkaai
Pandreitje
Waalse
Haanstraat
Steenstraat
St.-Niklaasstr.
Oude Zakstr.
Wollestraat
Kartuizerinnenstr.
Eekhoutstr.
Geerolfstr.
Gevangenis
Kopstraat
Giststraat
Kernelstr.
Loppemstr.
Oude Burg
Diver
Eekhoutpoort
't Pand
Willemstr.
Zilverpand
Zilver steeg
Simon Stevinplein
Nieuwstr.
Grauthusestr.
Be ma
Zuidzandstr.
St.-Salvators-koorstr.
Pipersstr.
Guido Gezelleplein
Hof Arents
Groeninge
Lendestr.
Korte Vulderstr.
H.-Geeststr.
Hoogste van Brugge
START
Goezeputstraat
Mariastraat
O.L.V.-kerkhof-Zuid
St.-Jan in de Meers
Bakkersstr.
OUD SINT-JAN
Congrescentrum
Koolbranderstr.
St.-Obrechtsstr.
Nieuwe Gen
Kastanjeboomstraat
Stoofstraat
Walstraat
Walplein
Driekroezenstr.
Zonnekemeers
Oude Gentweg
Werkhuisstraat

From Guido Gezelleplein to Markt

This square is named after the Flemish priest and poet Guido Gezelle (1830-1899). Take a seat on one of the square's benches and enjoy Gezelle's lovely statue and the side-view of the Church of Our Lady **15**. Its one hundred and twenty-two metres high brick tower is sure proof of the craftsmanship of Bruges' artisans. Take a look inside and admire the rich art collection that includes Michelangelo's world-famous Madonna and Child and the 15th- and 16th-century mausoleums of Mary of Burgundy and Charles the Bold. On your left is the striking residence of the lords of Gruuthuse, now the Gruuthusemuseum **24**. The tower and well were status symbols, and evidence of the Gruuthuse family's great wealth. They made their fortune from their exclusive rights on *gruut* (gruit), a herb mixture that, ages before hop, was used to flavour beer. Louis of Gruuthuse not only commanded the army of Charles

DID YOU KNOW?

In recent years the tower of the Church of Our Lady has become home to a pair of nesting peregrine falcons. These lightning-fast birds of prey are welcome guests, because they are the ideal weapon in the never-ending fight against the nuisance caused by… pigeons.

the Bold, he was also the personal bodyguard to Mary of Burgundy. A cultured man, he owned the Gruuthuse manu-

TIP

From 22 March 2013 the magnificent Gruuthuse manuscript can once again be admired in Bruges **24**. This valuable collection of medieval songs will be on loan for just a few months from the Royal Library in The Hague.
You read more on page 82.

script, a famous medieval codex containing amongst its many texts no fewer than 147 songs. The family's motto was *Plus est en vous* (There is more in you than you think). It's proudly displayed above the door of their residence.

Continue along the narrow footpath to the left of the church.
Look up immediately beyond the bend. Do you see the chapel that seems to hold the Gruuthuse Museum and the Church of Our Lady in a close embrace? As the lords of Gruuthuse were far too grand to mingle with the populace, they had their own private chapel high above the street, where they could follow Mass. This intimate place of worship can still be visited.

Retrace your steps, cross the attractive Gruuthuseplein and turn right into Dijver.
Number 12 is the Groeninge Museum 23 , Bruges' most famous museum. An interview with chief curator Till-Holger Borchert is on page 54. Further along Dijver is one of the locations of the College of Europe 03 , numbers 9-11, an international postgraduate institution that focuses on Europe.

Carry on down Dijver and turn left into Wollestraat.
Perez de Malvenda 13 is an impressive mansion on the corner of Wollestraat. This 15th-century town house, now a food shop, has been restored from attic to cellar. Just before Markt are the Cloth Halls 10 , the Belfry's 04 warehouses and sales outlets. Facing the street, countless stalls were selling all sorts of herbs for medicinal purpose and potions. Indeed, Bruges being an important trading centre could be by then import a variety of herbs from all over Europe.

Markt, Bruges' beating heart

Wollestraat leads to Markt.
Markt is dominated by its Belfry 04 , for centuries the city's foremost edifice and the perfect look-out in case of war, fire or any other calamity. You can still

THE CORRECT TIME

A gleaming terrestrial globe proudly sits on top of Boechoute, the house on the corner. This building from 1477 with its original lean-to-roof is now the Meridian 3 tearoom (on the Markt). When the Brussels to Bruges railway line was inaugurated, not all clocks in Belgium were set to the same time. The shortcoming was cured by the globe. At noon exactly the sun coincided with its shadow through a hole in the globe. The line that was thus drawn can still be traced today thanks to a string of copper nails.

Markt

climb to the top of the tower; but you will need to conquer no fewer than 366 steps to get there! Fortunately, there are a couple of places during your ascent where you can stop for a breather. Once at the top you will be rewarded with an unforgettable panoramic view.

At the foot of the Belfry are the world's most famous chippies ('frietkoten')! The statue of Jan Breydel and Pieter de Coninck graces the middle of the square. These two popular heroes of Bruges resisted French oppression and consequently played an important part

TIP

As you are climbing your way to the top of the belfry tower **04**, why not stop for a break at the vaulted treasure chamber, where the city's charters, seal and public funds were all kept during medieval times.

The drum

You can make a second stop at the 'Stenen Vloer' (Stone Floor): here you will learn everything you ever wanted to know about the clock, the drum and the carillon of 47 harmonious bells, which together weigh a staggering 27 tons of pure bronze. If you are really lucky, you might see the city's bell-ringer in action, banging on the wooden keys that make the bells sound

during the Battle of the Golden Spurs in 1302. Their statue neatly looks out onto the Gothic revival style Provincial Court (Markt 3) **18**. Until the 18th century this used to be the extremely busy Water-halle, a covered warehouse where goods were loaded and unloaded along the canals that ran alongside the square. Today the canals are still there, albeit underground. Would you like a break? Then treat yourself to a coach ride and explore the city by horse and carriage for half an hour. Or maybe you prefer a fifty-minute city tour by minibus? You can continue your walk after your trip.

From Markt to Jan van Eyckplein

Ignore Markt on your left and continue straight ahead to Vlamingstraat.

In the 15th century this used to be the harbour area's shopping street. A fair number of banks had a branch here, and wine taverns were two a penny. Each of these had a deep cellar where French and Renish wines could easily be stacked. In the medieval vaulted cellars of Taverne Curiosa (Vlamingstraat 20), the alcoholic atmosphere of those bygone days can still be inhaled. Halfway along Vlamingstraat is the elegant City Theatre **41** on your left. This royal theatre (1869) is one of Europe's best-preserved city theatres. Behind the eclectic façade lie a palatial auditorium and a regal foyer. Papageno, the bird seller from Mozart's opera, The Magic Flute, guards the entrance. His score lies scattered on the square opposite.

> TIP
>
> Since as long ago as 1897, two green-painted mobile chippies have stood in front of the Belfry. It is definitely the best place in town to buy – and sell – chips, good for the annual consumption of several tons of fast food! The city's chip-sellers can bid once every two years for the right to stand on this lucrative spot. The highest bidder gets the contract. The stalls are open nearly every hour of the day and night, so that you never need to go hungry!

SWANS ON THE CANALS

After the death of Mary of Burgundy, Bruges went through some troubled times. The townspeople, enraged by new taxes Maximilian of Austria, Mary's successor, had imposed upon them, rose in revolt against their new ruler. As Maximilian was locked up in House Craenenburg on the market square, he helplessly witnessed the torture and eventual beheading of his bailiff and trusted councillor Pieter Lanchals. According to legend, once the duke had regained power, the citizens of Bruges were ordered to keep swans or long necks ('langhalzen') on the canals for all eternity.

Continue along Vlamingstraat and turn right into Kortewinkel just before the canal.

Somewhat hidden from gazing eyes, Kortewinkel boasts a unique 16th-century wooden house front. It is one of only two left in the city (you will come across the other one further along this walk).

Just a few metres on is another delicious discovery at number 10. The Jesuit Monastery  has a magnificent secretive courtyard garden. Is its door open? Then walk in and enjoy its heavenly peace.

Kortewinkel turns into Spaanse Loskaai, the home port of the Spanish merchants in Burgundian times.

The picturesque bridge on your left is the Augustine Bridge, one of Bruges' oldest specimens, what with its seven hundred summers. The stone seats were originally intended to display the wares of the diligent sellers. The bridge affords an excellent view of the house in the right-hand corner, which connects Spanjaardstraat with Kortewinkel. This used to be not only a monastery but also a haunted house, so say the locals. When an amorous monk was rejected by a nun, the man murdered her and then committed suicide. Ever since they have been haunting that ramshackle building…

Continue along Spaanse Loskaai, go down the first street on your right and proceed to Oosterlingenplein.

During Bruges' Golden Age this was the fixed abode of the so-called 'Oosterlingen' or German merchants. Their imposing warehouse took up the entire left side of the square. Today the only remnant is the building to the right of Hotel Bryghia. Their warehouse must have been truly grand!

Beyond Oosterlingenplein is Woensdagmarkt. You will then find yourself on the square on which the statue of the painter Hans Memling attracts all attention. Turn right into Genthof.

Here the second of two authentic medieval wooden house fronts draws attention. Notice that each floor juts out a little more than the next one. This building technique, which helped to avoid water damage, was consequently used in various architectural styles.

Burgundian Manhattan

Proceed to Jan van Eyckplein.

This was Burgundian Bruges' Manhattan, the place to be! Here ships docked, cargoes were loaded and unloaded and tolls were levied. In this unremitting hustle and bustle a cacophony of languages was heard above the din, the one sounding even louder than the other. What a soundtrack! Each business transaction required a few local sounds too, of course, as there always had to be a Bruges broker present who would naturally pocket his cut. On the corner 16th-century Huis De Roode Steen has been sparkling in all its glory since its restoration in 1877. At numbers 1-2 is the Old Tollhouse (1477) **21** **06** , where all tollage was settled. To the left of this monumental building is Pijndershuisje, Bruges' narrowest dwelling. The house belonged to a *pijnder* or docker, a name that you can easily derive from its telling façade, that is if you keep your eyes peeled. The hunched 'pijnders' were employed to load and unload sacks and casks.

Continue along Academiestraat.

Right on the corner with Jan van Eyckplein is another remarkable construction, distinguished by its striking tower. This is Burghers' Lodge **15** , a kind of 15th-century private club where prominent inhabitants of Bruges could mix socially with foreign merchants. Hidden in a niche of this

> TIP
>
> The Genthof has in recent years attracted a variety of different arts and crafts. There is a glass-blower, a poetry shop, a trendy vintage store and a number of contemporary art galleries. And on the corner you can find 't Terrastje, the café with probably the smallest terrace in Bruges.

Burghers Lodge is the little Bruges' Bear, one of the city's most important symbols.

Proceed to Grauwwerkersstraat.
The little square connecting Academiestraat with Grauwwerkersstraat has been known as 'Beursplein' since time immemorial.
Here merchants were engaged in high-quality trade. The merchant houses of Genoa (later renamed 'Saaihalle' 08, and today Belgian Fries Museum 20), Florence (now De Florentijnen restaurant) and Venice (now De Slegte bookshop) once stood here side by side like brothers. In front of Huis ter Beurze (1276), the central inn 11, merchants from all over Europe used to gather to arrange business appointments and

conduct exchange transactions. The Dutch word for stock exchange became 'beurs', derived from the name of the house. Many other languages would take over this term, such as French (*bourse*) or Italian (*borsa*).

Turn into Grauwwerkersstraat and stop immediately in your tracks.
The side wall of Huis ter Beurze, and more precisely the part between the two sets of ground-floor windows, bears the signatures of the stonemasons. This way everybody knew which mason cut which stones and which mason remained to be paid. The house next-door to Huis ter Beurze, called the Little Beurze, still sits on its original street level.

THE LITTLE BEAR OF BRUGES

When Baldwin Iron Arm, the first Count of Flanders, visited Bruges for the first time, the first creature he saw was a big 'white' bear. According to legend, all this happened in the 9th century. After a fierce fight the count succeeded in killing the animal. In homage to the courageous beast he proclaimed the bear to be the city's very own symbol. Today the bear in the niche of the Burghers' Lodge is festively rigged out during exceptional celebrations. The Bruges Bear is holding the coat of arms of the Noble Company of the White Bear, which was a kind of jousting club for local knights, founded shortly after Baldwin's famous victory over the original 'white' bear.

Turn left into Naaldenstraat.
On your right, Bladelin Court **09** with its attractive tower looms up ahead. In the 15th century, treasurer of the Order of the Golden Fleece Pieter Bladelin, portrayed

above the gate whilst praying to the Virgin Mary, leased his house to the Florentine banking family of de Medici, who set up one of their branches here. Today the edifice belongs to the Sisters of Our Lady of Seven Sorrows. We highly recommend a visit. But make a reservation before you go, by phoning +32 (0)50 33 64 34 and admire the magnificent courtyard garden and the city's first Renaissance façade, embellished with two stone medallions representing Lorenzo de Medici and his wife Clarissa Orsini.

Somewhat further along, next to another ornamental tower, turn right into Boterhuis, a winding cobbled alley that catapults you back straight into the Middle Ages. Keep right, pass Saint James' Church and turn left into Moerstraat. The Dukes of Burgundy and the vast majority of foreign merchants patronised Saint James' Church **22**. Their extrava-

PRINSENHOF GOSSIP

> As Philip the Good hadn't yet laid eyes on his future wife, he sent Jan van Eyck to Portugal to paint her portrait. This way the duke wanted to make certain he had made the right choice. The duke's ploy worked, because history teaches us that the couple had a happy marriage.

> Although the popular Mary of Burgundy incurred only a minor fracture due to her fall off her horse, the accident would eventually lead to her death at Prinsenhof. Back in those times there was no cure for inflammation.

> During the recent hotel renovation no fewer than 568 silver coins, minted between 1755 and 1787, were dug up. After some careful counting and calculations it is assumed that the energetic English nuns entrusted the coins to the soil so as to prevent the advancing French troops from stealing their hard-earned capital.

gant gifts have left their glittering mark on the interior.

Prinsenhof (the Princes' Court), home base of the Dukes of Burgundy

Turn left into Geerwijnstraat and carry on to Muntplein.

Muntplein (Coin Square) belongs to nearby Prinsenhof 16 . As you might have guessed, this was where Bruges' mint was situated. The statue Flandria Nostra (Our

----

TIP

Behind the street Boterhuis, at Sint-Jakobsstraat 26, you will find Cinema Lumière 09 , purveyor of the better kind of artistic film. In other words, the place to be for real film-lovers.

Flanders), which represents a noblewoman on horseback, was designed by the Belgian sculptor Jules Lagae.

At the end of Geerwijnstraat turn right into Geldmuntstraat. The walk's finishing point is Prinsenhof.

We end the walk on a highlight. Prinsenhof used to be the palace of the counts and dukes. This impressive mansion, originally seven times the size of what you see today, was erected in the 15th century by Philip the Good to celebrate his (third) marriage to Isabella of Portugal. When Philip the Bold remarried Margaret of York, a swimming pool and a zoological garden were added to the ducal residence. It is no surprise that Prinsenhof not only became the favourite pied-à-terre of the Dukes of Burgundy, but also the nerve centre of their political, economic and cultural ambitions. Both Philip the Good (d.1467) and Mary of

Burgundy (d.1482) breathed their last here. After the death of the popular Mary of Burgundy the palace's fortunes declined, until it eventually ended up in private hands. In the 17th century, English nuns converted it into a boarding school for girls of well-to-do parents. After the nuns had gone, the complex changed ownership many times. Today Prinsenhof belongs to the Kempinski hotel chain, which turned it into Bruges' first five-star hotel.

TIP

Whoever wants to get a really good impression of the magnificence of this city castle **16** and its elegant gardens should follow the signs in the Ontvangersstraat to the hotel car park at at Moerstraat 46. Of course, you can always treat yourself – and your nearest and dearest – to a princely dinner in the restaurant of the Dukes' Palace Hotel: the perfect way to enjoy the grandeur and luxury of the complex.

» START	Choco-Story (Wijnzakstraat)
» DISTANCE	4 km
» FINISH	Café Vlissinghe in Blekersstraat

Walk 3

Strolling through silent Bruges

Although the parishes of Saint Anne and Saint Giles are known as places of great tranquillity, the fact that they are off the beaten track does not mean that the visitor will be short of adventure. How about a row of nostalgic windmills? Or perhaps some unpretentious working-class neighbourhoods or a couple of exclusive gentlemen's clubs? Will you be able to absorb all these impressions serenely? Don't worry. After the tour we invite you to catch your breath in Bruges' oldest cafe!

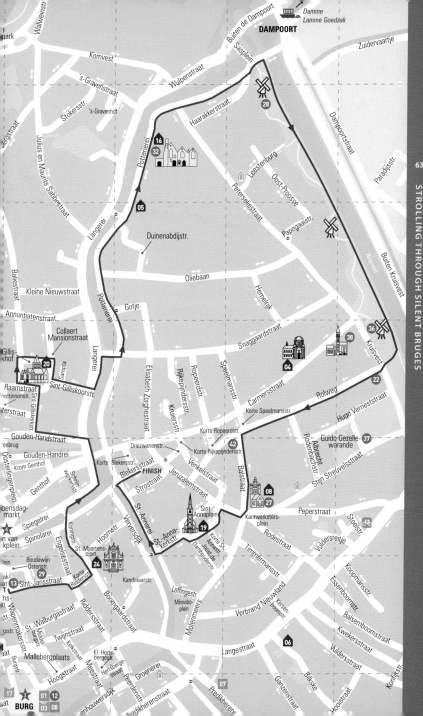

Damme
Lamme Goedzak

DAMPOORT

Buiten de Dampoort

Zuidervaartje

Komvest

's-Gravenstraat

Wulpenstraat

Sasplein

Stokerstr.

Haarakkerstraat

Dampoortstraat

28

's-Gravenhof

Paradijsstr.

Potterierei

16
32

Leestenburg

Oost-Proosse

Langerei

05

Peterseliestraat

Duinenabdijstr.

Buiten Kruisvest

Baliestraat

Kleine Nieuwstraat

Potterierei

Oliebaan

Hernelijk

Annuntiatenstraat

Gotje

Snaggaardstraat

36

Collaert
Mansionstraat

38

04

Gillis-
hof

20

Knusvest

Langerei

Elisabeth Zorghestraat

Rijkepijndersstr.

Ropeerdstr.

Speelmansstr.

Carmersstraat

22

Raamstraat

Sint-Gilliskoorstr.

Korte Speelmansstr.

Rolweg

nottinnenstr.

erstraat

Hugo Verriesstraat

Gouden-Handstraat

Kruelsstr.

Korte Ropeerdstr.

Guido Gezelle-
warande

37

enbrug

Gouden-Handrei

Driezwanenstr.

Korte Rijkepijndersstr.

42

Albrecht
Rodenbachstr.

Krom Genthof

Korte Blekersstr.

Oosterlingenplein

Genthof

Scharn-
werkstr.

Blekersstraat

FINISH

Venkelstraat

Jeruzalemstraat

Stijn Streuvelsstraat

oensdag-
markt

Spiegelrei

Strostraat

Balstraat

08

Peperstraat

Spinolarei

n van
kplein

St.-Annarei

27

Sloetr.

Vuldersreitje

St.-Maartens-
plein

Hoornstr.

Verversdijk

Sint
Annaplein

Kantwerksters-
plein

Koopmansstr.

Boudewijn
Ostenstr.

Konings.

19

Rodestraat

Timmermansstr.

29

St.-Anna-
kerkstr.

Essenboomstr.

13

Sint-Jansstraat

24

Korte
Riddersstr.

Korte St.
Annastraat
Boog de
Damhoudersstr.

Balsemboomstraat

Engelsestraat

Kandelaarstr.

Leffingestr.

Verbrand Nieuwland

Kersen-
boomstr.

Kwekersstraat

St.-Walburgastraat

Ridderstraat

Middel-
burgstr.

Twijnstraat

Boomgaardstraat

Minnebo-
plein

Molenmeers

Langestraat

06

Vulderstraat

Kl. Herts-
bergesstr.

Kelkstraat

Meestraat

Hertsberge-
straat

Groenerei

Komfitstr.

Mallebergplaats

Hoogstraat

Peerdenstr.

Hooistraat

Bikske

17
3

01 12
03 08

BURG

nhouwersdijk

Predikherenr.

07

Predikherenstraat

Ganzenstraat

From Choco-Story to Gouden-Handstraat

Choco-Story (museum of chocolate, Wijnzakstraat 2) **13** is the perfect starting point for the longest walk in this guide. This museum not only dips you in the yummy history of chocolate and cocoa, it also offers extensive chocolate tasting. If you wish, you can also buy your supplies here. No doubt the chocolate will help you to keep up a brisk pace! At the same address Lumina Domestica **29** contains the world's largest collection of lamps and lights. The museum also houses 6.000 antiques.

Turn left into Sint-Jansstraat, carry on to Korte Riddersstraat and turn left to Sint-Maartensplein.
Saint Walburgha's Church **24** rises up in all its magnificence right in front of you. This Baroque edifice (1619-1642) boasts a remarkable marble communion rail and high altar. In summer, glorious classical music recitals are offered free to church visitors. At number 4 is the erstwhile Scottish warehouse.

Continue down Koningstraat to the bridge.
This bridge, which connects poetic Spinolarei with Spiegelrei, affords a lovely view of Oud Huis Amsterdam on your left. Today this historic town house is an elegant hotel. This part of the city used to be mainly populated by the English and Scots. The English merchants even

TIP

The priest at the St. Walburga Church **24** regularly plays classical masterpieces on his church sound system. Listening to evocative concertos and sonatas as the twilight gathers in this ancient building, with the bats whirring silently just above your head: the perfect prelude to a magical summer evening in Bruges.

had their own steegere or stair where their goods were unloaded. The stair is still there, and the street connecting it is appropriately called Engelsestraat. The dignified white school building across the bridge was once a college of English Jesuits.

Saint Giles's, home base of workmen and artists

Cross the bridge, turn right along Spiegelrei and turn into Gouden-Handstraat, the fourth street on your left.

In the 15th century Gouden-Handstraat and the parish of Saint Giles were known as the artists' quarter. Hans Memling may have lived a few streets further down in Sint-Jorisstraat, the fact of the matter is that Jan van Eyck had a studio in Gouden-Handstraat, and that his somewhat lesser known fellow artists also used to congregate in this neighbourhood.

Turn right into Sint-Gilliskerkstraat. This street bumps into Saint Giles's Church **20** in the heart of the tranquil quarter of Saint Giles's. Initially a chapel, this house of God was upgraded to a par-

ish church in 1258. In spite of its interior in Gothic revival style and its superb paintings, the church takes on the appearance of a simple, sturdy village church. Don't be misled. In and around the church countless famous painters were buried, such as Hans Memling (d.1494), in his time the best paid painter, Lanceloot Blondeel (d.1561) and Pieter Pourbus (d.1564). Their graves and the cemetery may have disappeared, but their artists' souls still hover in the air.

Walk around the church and turn into Sint-Gilliskoorstraat.

Although the workmen's dwellings in these streets are rather small, they nevertheless display a bricked up window. As it happened, a tax on windows was levied in 1800. As a consequence,

BRUGES AND THE SEA

For centuries, Potterierei ensured the city's wealth. This canal ran to Damme where it was connected to a large lock, called 'Speie', which in turn was connected to the Zwin, a deep sea channel and tidal inlet. While Damme developed into an outport, Bruges grew into Northwestern Europe's greatest business centre of the Middle Ages. The arts flourished, culture thrived, prosperity seemed to be set for all eternity. The tide turned when Mary of Burgundy suddenly passed away. The relations between Bruges and the Burgundians turned sour and the Burgundian court left the city. The foreign merchants and their wealth followed in its wake. The Zwin silted up and Bruges lost her privileged commercial position. The city thus fell into a deep winter sleep.

a large number of windows were walled up.

From Potterierei to the vesten (ramparts)

Turn left into Langerei at the end of the street. Cross lovely Snaggaardbrug, the first bridge you get to, and turn left into Potterierei. You will have to follow the canal for some time.

After a fair distance along Potterierei is Bruges' Major Seminary at number 72 **05** on your right. A unique place with a lush orchard and meadows with cows at pasture. Between 1628 and 1642 a new Cistercian Abbey was erected here, which later on would achieve great fame for the wealth and erudition of its occupants. During the French Revolution, the abbey was brought under public ownership, and the abbot and monks were chased away. The 17th-century abbey buildings were first used as a military hospital and then as a military depot

and a grammar school before they were eventually taken over by the Major Seminary in 1833. Up to the present day the Seminary has been training catholic priests here. Just a few yards further down at number 79 is Our Lady of the Pottery **32** **16**. Its history goes back to the 13th century. Diligent nuns used to treat pilgrims, travellers and the sick here. The Gothic church with its Baroque interior and its rich collection of works of art, accumulated by the hospital throughout the centuries, is a hidden gem that is certainly well worth a visit!

05

Carry on to the lock and turn right. This idyllic spot is where the canal Damse Vaart heads out across the other side of the ring road towards the equally romantic town of Damme. It's hard to believe that this area around the canal was once a scene of great controversy. Up until the Eighty Years' War, Bruges was connected to Sluis by way of Damme. Ambitious Napoleon Bonaparte had the link with the tidal inlet of the Zwin, the natural predecessor of the Damse Vaart, dredged by Spanish prisoners of war so as to create a watercourse that would run all the way to Antwerp. His plan then was to develop the port city of Antwerp into a naval base, which would enable him to avoid the English sea blockade. Napoleon's project left Damme cut in twain, even if the wild plans of the Little General were never fully realised. When Belgium became independent in 1830, the new au-

TIP

Have we made you curious? Or do you just like to do things the easy way? If so, leave your bike and car at home and 'all aboard' for a voyage on the Lamme Goedzak 🚢, the most stylish way to reach the town of Damme. Step back in time during this nostalgic journey along Napoleon's canal.

thorities stopped the project, which in the end would go no further than Hoeke, one of Damme's boroughs. Today the low-traffic bicycle path skirting the canal is a most attractive route linking Bruges with Damme. The trip is highly recommended, as it traverses le plat pays, that flat country made famous by Jacques Brel in the moving song of that name. Imagine! In the middle of a unique polder landscape this truly poetic canal strip, bordered by

THE ARCHERS' GUILD: 165 MEN AND 1 QUEEN!

Although this used to be one of the poorer areas of the city for a very long time, the district includes two exclusive clubs. A greater contradiction cannot be found! Are you sitting comfortably out of harm's way on the slope of Sint-Janshuis Mill **36**? Then look down on your left. There is Saint George's Guild **37**, a fellowship of crossbow men. Down on your right is Saint Sebastian's Guild **38** with its remarkably elegant tower. This guild goes back more than six centuries, which makes it unique in the world. The society numbers 165 male members exactly and one notable female member: the Queen of England. Ever since the exiled English king Charles II took up residence in Bruges in the 17th century, the city and the British Royal Family have always been closely associated. Whenever the British Royal Family is on a state visit to Belgium, so the rumour goes, they first of all pop in at the Saint Sebastian's Archers' Guild.

lofty poplars bended down by eternal westerly winds.

Turn right and carry on along the Vesten (canals), which surround the city like a ring of green.
In the 16th century more than thirty windmills were turning their sails here. Today only four are left. In the 18th century the millers stood by helplessly when bread consumption took a dive and people started to consume more potatoes. Eventually steam machines would take over the millers' tasks. The Koelewei Mill **28** and Sint-Janshuis Mill **36** are open to

visitors. The miller will happily explain the workings of his mill, and he will gladly give a milling demonstration, too. Make sure you climb the slope upon which Sint-Janshuis Mill (the third mill) is standing! The hill affords a fantastic panoramic view of the city. This is the perfect spot to brush up on your amassed knowledge of Bruges. And there's more! Down below on your right is Verloren Hoek (the Lost Corner), now an authentic working-class district, but back in the 19th century an impoverished neighbourhood with such a bad reputation that even the police didn't dare enter its streets.

Silent Bruges

Descend down the slope and turn right into Rolweg.

Right on the corner is the Gezelle Museum **22**, the birthplace of Guido Gezelle (1830-1899), one of Flanders' most venerable poets. On display are handwritten letters, writing material and a deliciously peaceful garden with an age-old Corsican pine. Gezelle's parents worked here as gardener and caretaker, in exchange for which, they and their family received free board and lodgings. Little Guido grew up in these idyllic surroundings. He would eventually return to Bruges many years later and after many a peregrination. Upon his return he became curate of Saint Walburgha's Church. He also took over the running of the English Convent **04** (Carmersstraat 83-85), where he would die. These were his last words, reportedly: 'I have so loved hearing the birds singing.' Here, in this most verdant part of Bruges, we still know precisely what the priest and poet meant.

> TIP
>
> Interested in a little something 'extra'? Then go and take a look at the Albrecht Rodenbachstraat, another of the city's hidden gems. This green suburb *avant la lettre* offers an almost unbroken succession of step-gables and other fascinating facades, each fronted by a delightful little garden.

Turn into Balstraat, the second street on the left.

This picturesque working-man's alley houses the Folklore Museum **42**. The 17th-century row of single-room dwellings, restored and converted into authentic artisans' interiors such as a milliner's, a confectioner's and a small classroom, will take you back to bygone days. The tower of the 15th-century Jerusalem Chapel **08** can easily be spotted from

these premises. This chapel was commissioned by the Adornes, a prominent Bruges merchant family of Genovese origin. In 1470 Anselm Adornes collected one of his sons (the father had no fewer than sixteen children) in Padua before setting off on a pilgrimage to the Holy Land. Upon his return to Bruges Anselm

decided to build an exact copy of the Church of the Holy Sepulchre. The result can be said to be remarkable, indeed! Next door to the chapel is the Lace Centre 27. Here the young as well as the more experienced can take workshops as well as quick courses. The lace centre has its own museum and up until fifty years ago, the row of restored alms houses was inhabited by lace-makers. If you enter the museum during a lace-making demonstration, then it will seem like you have gone back in time.

At the crossroads turn right into Jeruzalemstraat, then, at the church, left onto Sint-Annaplein.
The tiny square is dominated by the ap-

TIP

If you feel like taking a break, you are welcome to rest your tired feet in the large, walled garden of the Folklore Museum 42. It is a delightful oasis of calm in the heart of the city, and even has its own outdoor bowling alley!

yourself down on a shady bench and enjoy this exceptional prospect.

Retrace your steps for just a few yards and turn right into Blekersstraat next to the bridge.

Café Vlissinghe at number 2 is undoubtedly Bruges' oldest café. This has been a tavern since 1515. It is no surprise then that you will find oodles of ambiance here. It is therefore the perfect place to settle down and let the wonderful memories of your walk slowly sink in. A local beer will be your ideal companion. Cheers!

parently simple Church of Saint Anne 19. Her exterior may be austere, her interior on the other hand is one of Bruges' most splendid examples of Baroque architecture. If you are lucky, you might be able to catch a glimpse of this interior – notwithstanding the restoration work that is currently taking place. As this neighbourhood gradually became more upmarket, naturally the church did the same!

With the church behind you turn left into Sint-Annakerkstraat and then right into Sint-Annarei.

At the corner of the confluence of the two waterways one of Bruges' most handsome town houses is proudly showing off its Rococo credentials. Sit

Know your way around Bruges

Bruges museums and places of interest

Some places are so special, so breathtaking or so unique that you simply have to see them. Bruges is filled to the brim with wonderful witnesses of a prosperous past. Although the Flemish Primitives are undoubtedly Bruges' showpiece attraction, museum devotees in search of much more will not be disappointed. Indeed, the Bruges range of attractions is truly magnificent. From modern plastic art by way of Michelangelo's world-famous 'Madonna and Child' to a sumptuous Burgundian palace. It's all there for you to discover!

🏛 ♿ (ground floor) **01**

Archeologiemuseum (Archaeological Museum)

This museum presents the unwritten history of Bruges. Its motto: feel your past beneath your feet. Discover the history of the city through different kinds of search and hands-on activities. A fascinating mix of archaeological finds, riddles, replicas and reconstructions shed light on daily life in times gone by, from the home to the workplace and from birth till death.

OPENENING TIMES > Tuesday to Sunday: 9.30 a.m.-12.30 p.m. and 1.30 p.m.-5.00 p.m.; last tickets: 12.00 p.m. and 4.30 p.m. (Open on Easter Monday and Whit Monday)

ADDITIONAL CLOSING DATES > 1/1, 9/5 (afternoon) and 25/12

ADMISSION > € 4.00; 65+: € 3.00; children under 13: free; youngsters under 26: € 3.00; Brugge City Card: free

INFORMATION > Mariastraat 36a, www.museabrugge.be

🏛 **02 Arentshuis**

In this elegant 18th-century town house with its picturesque garden the work of the versatile British artist Frank Brangwyn (1867-1956) is on display on the top floor. Brangwyn's talent as an architect, painter and designer of glassware, furniture and jewellery is breathtaking. The ground floor is the setting for temporary plastic art exhibitions.

OPENENING TIMES > Tuesday to Sunday: 9.30 a.m.-5.00 p.m.; last tickets: 4.30 p.m. (Open on Easter Monday and Whit Monday)

ADDITIONAL CLOSING DATES > 1/1, 9/5 (afternoon) and 25/12

ADMISSION > € 4.00; 65+: € 3.00; children under 13: free; youngsters under 26: € 3.00; combination ticket with Groeninge Museum possible; Brugge City Card: free

INFORMATION > Dijver 16, www.museabrugge.be

🏛 ♿ (ground floor) **01**

Basiliek van het Heilig Bloed (Basilica of the Holy Blood)

This double chapel consists of the Romanesque Church of Saint Basil (1139-1149) on the ground floor and the Basilica on the first floor, rebuilt in Gothic revival style in the 19th century. The Relic of the Holy Blood is kept in the Basilica.

OPENENING TIMES > 15 October-31 March: 10.00 a.m.-12.00 a.m. and 2.00 p.m.-5.00 p.m.; 1 April- 14 October: 9.30 a.m.-12.00 a.m. and 2.00 p.m.-5.00 p.m.

ADDITIONAL CLOSING DATES > 15 October-31 March: Wednesday afternoon

ADMISSION > Double chapel: free; Treasure-chamber: € 2.00; students: € 1.50; children under 13 and; Brugge City Card: free

INFORMATION > Burg 13, www.holyblood.org

02 02 03 Begijnhof (Beguinage)

The 'Princely Beguinage Ten Wijngaarde' with its whitewashed house fronts, tranquil convent garden and beguinage museum was founded in 1245. Today the nuns of the Order of Saint Benedict inhabit the site. The Beguinage entrance gate closes without fail at 6.30 p.m.

OPENENING TIMES > Beguinage: daily 6.30 a.m.-6.30 p.m.; Beguine's house: Monday to Saturday, 10.00 a.m.-5.00 p.m., Sunday 2.30 p.m.-5.00 p.m.

ADMISSION > Beguinage: free; Beguine's house: € 2.00; youngsters: € 1.00; 60+: € 1.50; Brugge City Card: free

INFORMATION > Begijnhof 24-28-30, www.monasteria.org

04 Belfort (Belfry)

The most important of Bruges' towers stands 83 metres tall. It houses a treasure-chamber, an impressive clock mechanism and a carillon with 47 silvertoned bells. Last year the tower – the symbol of Bruges – was given a major face-lift. In the reception area, waiting visitors can now discover all kinds of interesting information about the history and working of this unique world-heritage protected belfry. Those who take on the challenge of climbing

the tower can pause for a breather on the way up in the old treasure-chamber, where the city's charters, seal and public funds were kept during the Middle Ages, and also at the level of the clock or in the bell-ringer's chamber. Finally, after a tiring 366 steps, your efforts will be rewarded with a breathtaking and unforgettable panoramic view of Bruges and her surroundings.

OPENENING TIMES > Daily: 9.30 a.m.-5.00 p.m.; last tickets: 4.15 p.m.

ADDITIONAL CLOSING DATES >
1/1, 9/5 (afternoon) and 25/12

ADMISSION > € 8.00; 65+: € 6.00; children under 7: free; youngsters under 26: € 6.00; Brugge City Card: free

INFORMATION > Markt 7, www.museabrugge.be

NEW
Brouwerij 'Bourgogne des Flandres' (Brewery)

Since 1765 the Van Houtryve family has been brewing beer that is worthy of the dukes of Burgundy. Seven generations later, Bourgogne des Flandres beers are again being brewed in Bruges. What's more, they are being made according to a unique, centuries-old brewing technique: the infusion of lambic. This is a process that mixes a selection of the very best lambics with a brown beer of high fermentation. The Bourgogne des Flandres city brewery will open its doors in the summer of 2013. Expert guides will pilot visitors through centuries of beer history and at the end of the tour you can even try out the beer for yourself.

OPEN > From summer 2013. The exact times of opening can be found on the brewery website.

INFORMATION > Kartuizerinnenstraat 6, www.bourgognedesflandres.be

🏙❤ 11 Brouwerij 'De Halve Maan' (Brewery)

De Halve Maan (1546) is the oldest active brewery in the historic city centre of Bruges. Their house brew is *Brugse Zot*, a spirited top-fermented beer made from malt, hops and special yeast. This deliciously refreshing beer can be tasted on the premises. Daily guided tours in various languages.

OPENENING TIMES > April-October: daily 11.00 a.m.-4.00 p.m. (Saturday till

5.00 p.m.), guided tours every hour; November-March: weekdays 11.00 a.m. & 3.00 p.m., Saturday and Sunday 11.00 a.m.-4.00 p.m., guided tours every hour

ADDITIONAL CLOSING DATES > 1/1, 7/1-11/1, 14/1-18/1, 21/1-25/1, 24/12 and 25/12

ADMISSION > € 7.00 (including refreshment); children between 6 and 12: € 3.50; Brugge City Card: free

INFORMATION > Walplein 26, tel. +32 (0)50 44 42 22, www.halvemaan.be

🏙❤♿ 12 01 📷 08 Brugse Vrije (Liberty of Bruges)

From this mansion, erected between 1722 and 1727, Bruges' rural surroundings were governed. The building functioned as a court of justice between 1795 and 1984. Today the city archives are stored here. They safeguard Bruges' written memory. The premises also boast an old assize court and a renaissance hall with a monumental 16th-century timber, marble and alabaster mantelpiece.

OPENENING TIMES > Daily: 9.30 a.m.-12.30 p.m. and 1.30 p.m.-5.00 p.m.; last tickets: 12.00 p.m and 4.30 p.m.

ADDITIONAL CLOSING DATES >
1/1, 9/5 (afternoon) and 25/12
ADMISSION > Including City Hall and audio guide: € 4.00; 65+: € 3.00; children under 13: free; youngsters under 26: € 3.00; Brugge City Card: free
INFORMATION > Burg 11a,
www.museabrugge.be

13 Choco-Story (Chocolate Museum)

The museum dips its visitors in the history of cocoa and chocolate. From the Maya and the Spanish conquistadores to the chocolate connoisseurs of today. A chocolate hunt gives children the chance to discover the museum. Chocolates are made by hand and sampled on the premises.

OPENENING TIMES > Daily: 10.00 a.m.-5.00 p.m.; last tickets: 4.15 p.m.
ADDITIONAL CLOSING DATES >
1/1, 7/1-18/1, 24, 25 and 31/12
ADMISSION > € 7.00; 65+ and students: € 6.00; children between 6 and 12: € 4.00; children under 6: free; Brugge City Card: free
INFORMATION > Wijnzakstraat 2,
www.choco-story.be

15 Museum-Gallery Xpo Salvador Dalí

Admire the fantastic collection of world-famous graphic art, sculptures and drawings by the renowned Salvador Dalí inside the Belfry. All works are originals without a fault, authenticated by the Fundació Gala-Salvador Dalí. The collection is presented in a sensational Daliesque decor of mirrors and shocking pink.

OPENENING TIMES > Daily: 10.00 a.m.-6.00 p.m.
ADDITIONAL CLOSING DATES >
1/1 and 25/12
ADMISSION > € 10.00; 65+ and students: € 8.00; children under 12: free; Brugge City Card: free
INFORMATION > Markt 7,
www.dali-interart.be

18 Diamantmuseum Brugge (Bruges Diamond Museum)

This museum illustrates the history of Bruges as the oldest diamond centre in Europe. Today diamond remains one of Belgium's most important export products. The daily demonstration of diamond cutting is a sparkling affair.

OPENENING TIMES > Daily, 10.30 a.m.-
5.30 p.m. The diamond cutting shows
begin at 12.15 p.m. and 3.15 p.m. during
the weekends and school holidays, daily
during the period 1/2-31/10. At 12.15 p.m.
only on weekdays during the period
1/11-31/3. (Your presence is required
15 minutes in advance.)

ADDITIONAL CLOSING DATES >
1/1, 7/1-18/1, 24/12 and 25/12

ADMISSION > Museum: € 7.00; museum
+ diamond cutting demonstration:
€ 10.00; Brugge City Card: free

INFORMATION > Katelijnestraat 43,
www.diamondmuseum.be

⓾ 20 Frietmuseum (Belgian Fries Museum)

This didactical museum sketches the
history of the potato, Belgian fries and
the various sauces and dressings that
accompany this most delicious and
most famous of Belgian comestibles.
The museum is housed in Saaihalle, one
of Bruges' most attractive buildings.

OPENENING TIMES > Daily: 10.00 a.m.-
5.00 p.m.; last tickets: 4.15 p.m.

ADDITIONAL CLOSING DATES >
1/1, 7/1-18/1, 24, 25 and 31/12

ADMISSION > € 6.00; 65+ and students:
€ 5.00; children between 6 and 12: € 4.00;
children under 6: free; Brugge City Card:
free

INFORMATION > Vlamingstraat 33,
www.frietmuseum.be

🎴 07 21 Gentpoort (Gate of Ghent)

The Gate of Ghent is one of four remaining medieval city gates. An entrance for foreigners, a border with the outside world for the townspeople of Bruges. The gate was a part of the city's defences as well as a passageway for the movement of produce and merchandise.

OPENENING TIMES > Thursday to Sunday: 9.30 a.m.-12.30 p.m. and 1.30 p.m.-5.00 p.m.; last tickets: 12.00 p.m. and 4.30 p.m.

ADDITIONAL CLOSING DATES > 1/1, 9/5 (afternoon) and 25/12

ADMISSION > € 4.00; 65+: € 3.00; children under 13: free; youngsters under 26: € 3.00; Brugge City Card: free

INFORMATION > Gentpoortvest, www.museabrugge.be

🎴 22 Gezelle Museum

This museum, dedicated to the life and work of Guido Gezelle (1830-1899), is incorporated in the house where the famous Flemish poet was born. The museum doesn't only focus on the life and oeuvre of the great Flemish poet, it also houses temporary exhibitions on creative writing. Adjacent to the house is a romantic garden, where Jan Fabre's *The Man Who Gives Fire* is bound to catch your eye.

OPENENING TIMES > Tuesday to Sunday: 9.30 a.m.-12.30 p.m. and 1.30 p.m.-5.00 p.m.; last tickets 12.00 p.m. and 4.30 p.m. (Open on Easter Monday and Whit Monday)

ADDITIONAL CLOSING DATES > 1/1, 9/5 (afternoon) and 25/12

ADMISSION > € 4.00; 65+: € 3.00; children under 13: free; youngsters under 26: € 3.00; Brugge City Card: free

INFORMATION > Rolweg 64,
www.museabrugge.be

🏙♿ 23 Groeningemuseum (Groeninge Museum)

The Groeninge Museum offers a varied overview of the history of Belgian plastic arts. Although the Flemish Primitives are a high point, you will also marvel at top 18th and 19th-century neoclassical pieces, masterpieces from Flemish Expressionism and post-war modern art.

OPENENING TIMES > Tuesday to Sunday: 9.30 a.m.-5.00 p.m.; tickets till 4.30 p.m. (Open on Easter Monday and Whit Monday)

ADDITIONAL CLOSING DATES > 1/1, 9/5 (afternoon) and 25/12

ADMISSION > Including Arentshuis: € 8.00; 65+ and youngsters under 26: € 6.00; children under 13: free; Brugge City Card: free

INFORMATION > Dijver 12,
www.museabrugge.be

🏙 24 Gruuthusemuseum (Gruuthuse Museum)

A royal welcome awaits you at this opulent city palace of the lords of Gruuthuse. The museum contains all manner of objects that shed light on everyday life between the 15th and 19th centuries. One of the major attractions is the Hall of Honour with its tapestries, impressive fireplace and richly decorated rafters, all witnessing the wealth and affluence of the lords of Gruuthuse.

OPENENING TIMES > Tuesday to Sunday: 9.30 a.m.-5 p.m.; last tickets: 4.30 p.m. (Open on Easter Monday and Whit Monday)

ADDITIONAL CLOSING DATES > 1/1, 9/5 (afternoon) and 25/12

ADMISSION > € 8.00; 65+: € 6.00; children

under 13: free; youngsters under 26:
€ 6.00; Brugge City Card: free
INFORMATION > Dijver 17,
www.museabrugge.be
From 22/3-23/6 the Gruuthuse Museum
will host an exhibition on the 'Gruuthuse
manuscript'. Read more on page 108, in the
interview with Brody Neuenschwander.

NEW

Historium Bruges

The Historium catapults you back to Bruges' Golden Age. Special effects, moving
pictures and pieces of scenery breathe life
into the year 1435. A thrilling love story
awaits you (which you can listen to in your
own language on the audio-guide): take a
walk around the port of medieval Bruges,
take a look in the studio of the great painter Jan van Eyck and inhale the atmosphere of the city's streets. Let yourself be
shocked and amused by the exotic fra-
grances and bawdy laughter in the bath
house or take a spectacular flight over
medieval Bruges. Afterwards, you can re-
live your experiences in the Duvelorium, a
beer-concept store that has a breathtaking panorama of the Markt.

OPEN > Daily from 10.00 a.m. – 6.00 p.m
(last tickets at 5.00 p.m.); on Thursday,
late opening until 9.00 p.m. (last tickets
at 8.00 p.m.)

ADDITIONAL CLOSING DATES > 1/1 and 25/12

ADMISSION > Including audio-guide:
€ 11.00; children 14 years and younger:
€ 5.50; Family Pass (2 adults and max.
3 children 14 years or younger): € 30.00;
combi-ticket Historium-Groeninge Museum: € 15.00; Brugge City Card: € 8.25

INFORMATION > Markt 1,
www.historium.be

09 Hof Bladelin
(Bladelin Court)

In around 1440 Pieter Bladelin, treasurer
of the Order of the Golden Fleece, commissioned the construction of Bladelin

Court. In the 15th century the powerful Florentine banking family of De Medici set up a branch here. The stone medallion portraits of Lorenzo de Medici and his wife still grace the picturesque inner court, which was recently restored to its former glory.

OPENENING TIMES > Inner court, buildings and chapel: Monday to Friday 9.00 a.m.-12.00 a.m. and 2.00 p.m.-5.00 p.m.; visits are only possible with a guide and by appointment, tel. +32 (0)50 33 64 34

ADDITIONAL CLOSING DATES >
during the weekend; public holidays

ADMISSION > Inner court, rooms and chapel: € 5.00

INFORMATION > Naaldenstraat 19

27 Kantcentrum (Lace Centre)

The Lace Centre is housed in the 15th-century complex housing a.o. historic almshouses funded by the Adornes family, who were also responsible for building the Jerusalem Chapel. Lace demonstrations (2.00 p.m.-5.00 p.m.) and a number of courses are regularly given in the lace workshop. The shop sells all kinds of lace paraphernalia.

OPENENING TIMES > Monday to Saturday: 10.00 a.m.-5.00 p.m.

ADDITIONAL CLOSING DATES >
1/1, 25/12 and public holidays

ADMISSION > (with or without guide) € 3.00; 65+, students (with student card) and children between 7 and 12: € 2.00; children under 7: free; Brugge City Card: free

INFORMATION > Peperstraat 3a, www.kantcentrum.eu

🏛 ㉙ Lumina Domestica (Lamp Museum)

The museum contains the world's largest collection of lamps and lights. More than 6.000 antiques tell the complete story of interior lighting. From torch and paraffin lamp to light bulb and LED.

OPENENING TIMES > Daily: 10.00 a.m.-5.00 p.m.; last tickets: 4.15 p.m.

ADDITIONAL CLOSING DATES > 1/1, 7/1-18/1, 24, 25 and 31/12

ADMISSION > € 6.00; 65+ and students: € 5.00; children between 6 and 12: € 4.00; children under 6: free; Brugge City Card: free

INFORMATION > Wijnzakstraat 2, www.luminadomestica.be

🏛 ♿ 🔺 15 ㉛ Onze-Lieve-Vrouwekerk (Church of Our Lady)

The 122 metres high brick tower of the Church of Our Lady is a perfect illustration of the craftsmanship of Bruges' artisans. The church displays a valuable art collection: Michelangelo's world-famous Madonna and Child, countless paintings, 13th-century painted sepulchres and the tombs of Mary of Burgundy and Charles the Bold.

OPENENING TIMES > Church and museum: Monday to Saturday: 9.30 a.m.-5.00 p.m. (tickets for the museum section are on sale in the south transept until 4.30 p.m.); Sunday and Holy Days: 1.30 p.m.-5.00 p.m. (last tickets 4.30 p.m.). The church and the museum are not open to the public during nuptial and funeral masses. Useful to know: restoration work is currently being carried out in the church.

ADDITIONAL CLOSING DATES >
Museum: 1/1, 9/5 (afternoon) and 25/12
ADMISSION > € 6.00; 65+: € 5.00; children under 13: free; youngsters under 26: € 5.00; Brugge City Card: free
INFORMATION > Mariastraat, www.museabrugge.be

16 32 Onze-Lieve-Vrouw-ter-Potterie (Our Lady of the Pottery)

This hospital dates back to the 13th century, when nuns took on the care of pilgrims, travellers and the sick. Over the centuries, the hospital developed into a modern home for the elderly. The hospital wards with their valuable collection of works of art, monastic and religious relics and a range of objects used in nursing have been converted into a museum. The Gothic church with its baroque interior can also be visited.

OPENENING TIMES > Tuesday to Sunday: 9.30 a.m.-12.30 p.m. and 1.30 p.m.-5.00 p.m.; last tickets: 12.00 p.m. and

4.30 p.m. (Open on Easter Monday and Whit Monday)
ADDITIONAL CLOSING DATES >
1/1, 9/5 (afternoon) and 25/12
ADMISSION > € 4.00; 65+ and youngsters under 26: € 3.00; children under 13: free; Brugge City Card: free
INFORMATION > Potterierei 79 B, www.museabrugge.be

17 Onze-Lieve-Vrouw-van-Blindekenskapel (Chapel of our Lady of the Blind)

The Chapel of Our Lady of the Blind is supposed to have been erected in timber in 1305 through the agency of Robert of Bethune, Count of Flanders. The count had the chapel built after the Battle of Mons-en-Pévèle (1304) in gratitude for the Virgin Mary. The present chapel dates from 1651. The miraculous oaken image of Our Lady of the Blind is a Madonna and Child from 1415. Each year on 15 August the procession of Our Lady of the Blind winds its way through the streets of Bruges. In order to abide by the *Solemn Oath*, sworn during the battle of Mons-en-Pévèle, the citizens

of Bruges have been devoting a so-called solemn oath-candle in the Church of Our Lady of the Pottery since 1304.

OPENENING TIMES > Daily: 9.00 a.m.-5.00 p.m.

INFORMATION > Kreupelenstraat

🎫 ㉞ Expo Picasso

The historic area of the former Hospital of Saint John (Old Saint John's) hosts a permanent exhibition of more than 120 original works of art by Pablo Picasso. Admire the engravings and rare illustrations as well as the drawings and ceramics of the world-famous artist. The exhibition outlines the evolution in his work: from his Spanish period to cubism to surrealism. Works by some of his artist friends such as Matisse, Miró, Braque, Rodin, Chagall and Ensor are also on display.

OPENENING TIMES > Daily: 10.00 a.m.-5.00 p.m., closed on Tuesdays but not during school holidays

ADDITIONAL CLOSING DATES > January and 25/12

ADMISSION > € 8.00; 60+ and youngsters between 7 and 18: € 6.00; children under 7: free; combination ticket Expo Picasso/

Museum-Gallery Xpo Salvador Dalí: € 15.00; 60+ and youngsters between 7 and 18: € 11.00; Brugge City Card: free

INFORMATION > Old Saint John's, Mariastraat 38, www.expo-brugge.be

🎫 ♿ ㉟ Sint-Janshospitaal (Saint John's Hospital)

Saint John's Hospital has an eight hundred-year-old history of caring for pilgrims, travellers and the sick. Visit the medieval wards where the nuns and monks performed their work of mercy and marvel at the impressive collection of archives, art works, medical instruments and six paintings by Hans Memling. Also worth a visit: the Diksmuide attic, the old dormitory, the custodian's room and the adjoining pharmacy.

OPENENING TIMES > Tuesday to Sunday: 9.30 a.m.-5.00 p.m.; last tickets: 4.30 p.m. The pharmacy is open from Tuesday to Sunday: 9.30 a.m.-11.45 a.m. and 2.00 p.m.-5.00 p.m.; last tickets: 4.30 p.m. (Open on Easter Monday and Whit Monday)

ADDITIONAL CLOSING DATES > 1/1, 9/5 (afternoon) and 25/12

ADMISSION > € 8.00; 65+ and youngsters

under 26: € 6.00; children under 13: free;
Brugge City Card: free

INFORMATION > Mariastraat 38,
www.museabrugge.be

🏠 36 Sint-Janshuismolen (Mill)
🏠 28 Koeleweimolen (Mill)

Windmills have graced Bruges' ramparts
ever since the construction of the outer
city wall at the end of the 13th century.
Today four specimen are left on Kruisvest. Sint-Janshuis Mill (1770) is still in its
original spot and still grinding grain just
like its neighbour Koelewei Mill.

OPENENING TIMES > Sint-Janshuis Mill:
May-August: Tuesday to Sunday,
9.30 a.m.-12.30 p.m. and 1.30 p.m.-
5.00 p.m.; last tickets 12.00 p.m. and
4.30 p.m. (Open on Whit Monday);

September: Saturday and Sunday,
9.30 a.m.-12.30 p.m. and 1.30 p.m.-
5.00 p.m.; last tickets 12.00 p.m. and
4.30 p.m. Koelewei Mill: July and August:
Tuesday to Sunday, 9.30 a.m.-12.30 p.m.
and 1.30 p.m.-5.00 p.m.; last tickets
12.00 p.m and 4.30 p.m.

ADDITIONAL CLOSING DATES >
Sint-Janshuis Mill: 9/5 (afternoon)

ADMISSION > € 3.00; 65+: € 2.00; children
under 13: free; youngsters under 26:
€ 2.00; Brugge City Card: free

INFORMATION > Kruisvest,
www.museabrugge.be

♿ 🏠 23 Sint-Salvatorskathedraal (Saint Saviour's Cathedral)

Bruges' oldest parish church (12th-15th
century) has amongst its treasures a

rood loft with organ, medieval tombs, Brussels tapestries and a rich collection of Flemish paintings (14th-18th century). The treasure-chamber displays a.o. paintings by Dieric Bouts, Hugo van der Goes and other Flemish Primitives. Useful to know: restoration work is currently being carried out in the church.

OPENENING TIMES > Cathedral: Monday to Friday: 9.00 a.m.-12.00 a.m. and 2.00 p.m.-5.30 p.m.; Saturday: 9.00 a.m.-12.00 a.m. and 2.00 p.m.-3.30 p.m.; Sunday: 9.00 a.m.-10.00 a.m. and 2.00 p.m.- 5.00 p.m.; Treasury: daily (except Saturday): 2.00 p.m.-5.00 p.m.

ADDITIONAL CLOSING DATES > Treasury: January

ADMISSION > Cathedral and Treasury: free

INFORMATION > Steenstraat, www.sintsalvator.be

38 Schuttersgilde Sint-Sebastiaansgilde (St. Sebastian's Archers Guild)

The Archers' Guild of Saint Sebastian goes back 600 years. A unique feat indeed! A visit includes the royal chamber, the chapel chamber and the garden.

OPENENING TIMES > 1 May-30 September: Tuesday, Wednesday and Thursday: 10.00 a.m.-12.00 a.m., Saturday: 2.00 p.m.-5.00 p.m. 1 October-30 April:

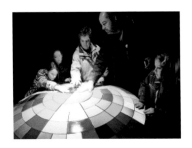

Tuesday, Wednesday, Thursday and Saturday: 2.00 p.m.-5.00 p.m.
ADMISSION > € 3.00
INFORMATION > Carmersstraat 174, www.sebastiaansgilde.be

🔲♿ 39 Sound Factory – Lantaarntoren

Why not pay a visit to the Sound Factory in the Lantaarntoren (Lantern Tower) at the Concertgebouw? Get to work with samples and sounds, and create your own compositions. The roof of the Lantaarntoren not only commands a unique view across the historic city centre, but gives you the opportunity to experiment with bells and sounds to your heart's content.
OPENENING TIMES > Tuesday to Sunday: 9.30 a.m.-5.00 p.m.; last tickets 4.30 p.m. (Open on Easter Monday and Whit Monday)
ADDITIONAL CLOSING DATES > 1/1, 9/5 (afternoon) and 25/12
ADMISSION > € 6.00; 65+: € 5.00; children under 13: free; youngsters under 26: € 5.00; Brugge City Card: free
INFORMATION > 't Zand 34, www.musea-brugge.be en www.sound-factory.be

🔲♿ 09 40 Stadhuis (City Hall)

Bruges' City Hall (1376) is one of the oldest in the Low Countries. It is from here that the city has been governed for more than 600 years. An absolute masterpiece is the Gothic Hall with its late 19th-century murals and polychrome vault. The adjoining historic hall calls up the city council's history with a number of authentic documents and works of art. A multimedia exhibition on the ground floor illustrates the evolution of the Burg square.
OPENENING TIMES > Daily: 9.30 a.m.-5.00 p.m.; last tickets: 4.30 p.m.
ADDITIONAL CLOSING DATES > 1/1, 9/5 (afternoon) and 25/12
ADMISSION > Including Liberty of Bruges and audio guide: € 4.00; 65+: € 3.00; children under 13: free; youngsters under 26: € 3.00; Brugge City Card: free
INFORMATION > Burg 12, www.museabrugge.be

🔲 42 Volkskundemuseum (Folklore Museum)

These restored 17th-century singleroom dwellings accommodate a.o. a classroom, a millinery, a pharmacy, a confectionery, a

grocery and an authentic bedroom. Conclude your visit with a pleasant stroll in the garden and a thirst-quenching drink at The Black Cat, the museum's tavern. Lace collection in the exhibition attic.

OPENENING TIMES > Tuesday to Sunday: 9.30 a.m.-5.00 p.m.; last tickets: 4.30 p.m. (Open on Easter Monday and Whit Monday)

ADDITIONAL CLOSING DATES > 1/1, 9/5 (afternoon) and 25/12

ADMISSION > € 4.00; 65+: € 3.00; children under 13: free; youngsters under 26: € 3.00; Brugge City Card: free

INFORMATION > Balstraat 43, www.museabrugge.be

WALLET-FRIENDLY MUSEUM SHOPPING!

» **Brugge City Card**

The Brugge City Card gives free entry to 26 museums and places of interest in Bruges. The Brugge City Card can be purchased at ℹ️ Markt (Historium), 't Zand (Concertgebouw) and Stationsplein (Station). See page 12 for more information.

» **Museum Pass**

With the Museum Pass you can visit the different Musea Brugge locations as often as you like for just € 20.00 (www.museabrugge.be). Young people (12 to 25 years of age) pay just € 15.00. The pass is valid for three consecutive days and can be purchased at all Musea Brugge locations and at ℹ️ 't Zand (Concertgebouw).

» **Combination ticket Choco-Story/Diamond Museum**

Combine a tasty visit to Choco-Story with a dazzling look at the Diamond Museum. This combination ticket costs € 12.00. For sale at the abovementioned museums and at ℹ️ 't Zand (Concertgebouw).

» **Combination ticket Choco-Story/Lumina Domestica/Belgian Fries Museum**

Visit these three museums at reduced rates.

» **Combination ticket (3 museums):** adults: € 16.00; 65+ and students: € 13.00; children between 6 and 12: € 9.00; children under 6: free

» **Combination ticket (select 2 museums):** adults: € 11.00; 65+ and students: € 9.00; children between 6 and 12: € 6.00; children under 6: free

» These combination tickets are for sale at the above-mentioned museums and at ℹ️ 't Zand (Concertgebouw).

Culture
and amusement

The city's high-quality cultural life flourishes as never before. Devotees of modern architecture stand in awe of the Concertgebouw (Concert hall) whilst enjoying to the full an international top concert or an exhilarating dance performance. Romantic souls throng the elegant City Theatre for an unforgettable night. Jazz enthusiasts feel at home at Art Centre De Werf, whereas MaZ is the place to be for young people.

🏙♿ 14 Concertgebouw (Concert Hall)

The impressive Concert Hall with its 1,295 seats and the intimate Chamber Music Hall with its 320 seats serve a delightful mix of music, musical theatre and dance of international quality. The acoustics and intimate comfort of both halls are exceptional. Brugge City Card: 30% discount on productions marked in the free monthly events@brugge magazine.

INFORMATION > 't Zand 34, tel. +32 (0)70 22 33 02 (Monday-Friday: 4.00 p.m.-6.30 p.m.), www.concertgebouw.be

🏙♿ 41 Stadsschouwburg (City Theatre)

One of Europe's best preserved city theatres (1869) boasts a palatial foyer and a majestic auditorium. It is the perfect setting for concerts and contemporary dance and theatre performances. Brugge City Card: 30% discount on productions marked in the free monthly events@brugge magazine.

INFORMATION > Vlamingstraat 29,

tel. +32 (0)50 44 30 60 (Weekdays 1.00 p.m.-6.00 p.m. Saturday 10.00 a.m.-1.00 p.m.), www.ccbrugge.be

🏙♿ 30 Magdalenazaal (MaZ, Magdalena Concert Hall)

The place to be for dynamic young theatre and dance talent as well as for concerts. Big names next to intimate club discoveries. Regular shows and activities for children. Brugge City Card: 30% discount on productions marked in the free monthly events@brugge magazine.

INFORMATION > Magdalenastraat 27, Sint-Andries, tel. +32 (0)50 44 30 60 (Weekdays 1.00 p.m.-6.00 p.m., Saturday 10.00 a.m.-1.00 p.m.), www.ccbrugge.be

🏙♿ 17 De Werf (Art Centre)

Celebrated den for jazz lovers. An established concert venue for countless Belgian and foreign musicians as well as a perfect spot for that enjoyable contemporary play or kids' production. A free jam session takes place in the foyer every second Monday of the month, and this from October through to May. Brugge City Card: 25% discount

INFORMATION > Werfstraat 108, tel. +32 (0)50 33 05 29, www.dewerf.be

What's on the programme?

The following list is a summary of the most important annual events in Bruges. At the info offices on the Markt (Historium), 't Zand (Concertgebouw) and the Stationsplein (station) you can pick up a free copy of **events@brugge** the monthly magazine of events in Bruges. And, of course, for a detailed events calendar you can always consult the website at http://events.brugge.be.

January

Bach Academie

For three days Bruges is under the spell of everything connected with the great Baroque composer from Leipzig. The Bruges Bach Academy focuses, together with Philippe Herreweghe and his Collegium Vocale Ghent, on the Bach oeuvre and on the St. Thomas cantorate in particular.

February

Brugs Bierfestival (Bruges Beer Festival)

For a full weekend the City Halls are the place to be if you want to learn more about Belgian beers, both old and new.
INFORMATION > www.brugsbierfestival.be
Read more in the interview with Bob Eck on page 132

Reismarkt (Travel Mart)

An alternative travel fair in the City Halls. Under the motto 'travellers help travellers', enthusiastic globetrotters exchange a wide range of tips and information about almost every type of travel and every destination you can think of.

March

Brugge Culinair (Culinary Bruges)

An exhibition for gourmets and gastronomes in the Oud-Sint-Jan complex. This year, for the first time, entrance is free.
INFORMATION > www.bruggeculinair.be

Ronde van Vlaanderen (Tour of Flanders)

This historic and world-famous race for professional cyclists will be contested for the 97th time in 2013. The start is on the Markt.
INFORMATION > www.rondevanvlaanderen.be
Read more in the interview with Marina Tasiopoulos on page 124

April

Mooov Festival

This 10-day film festival, screened in Cinema Lumière, shows the best new films from Africa, Asia and South America.
INFORMATION > tel. +32 (0)50 34 83 54, www.mooov.be

Erfgoeddag (Heritage Day)

Throughout Flanders hidden heritage gems open their doors to the general public. Each year there is a different theme.

INFORMATION > www.erfgoeddag.be

May

Meifoor (May Fair)

For four fun-filled weeks some 90 fairground attractions 'take over' 't Zand, the Beursplein, the Koning Albert Park and the Simon Stevinplein.

Ascension Day: Heilig Bloedprocessie (Procession of the Holy Blood)

First held in 1304, this popular procession through the streets of the city depicts scenes from the Old and New Testaments.

(Read more in the box text)

Dwars door Brugge (The Great Bruges Run)

Tens of thousands of runners set off on a 15-kilometre run through Bruges.

INFORMATION > www.brugge.be

June

Feest in 't Park (Party in the Park)

A free, family-friendly festival in the Minnewater Park, with a children's world village, workshops, world cooking and plenty of music, theatre and dance.

INFORMATION > www.feestintpark.be

Zandfeesten (Zand Festival)

Kilometres of antique and bric-a-brac stalls on 't Zand, attracting bargain-hunters from both near and far. (Most years the Zand Festival takes place at the beginning of July.)

A CENTURIES-OLD PROCESSION

Every year on Ascension Day, under the watchful eye of a huge public, the Holy Blood Procession passes through the streets of Bruges city centre. In the first two parts of the procession, members of the religious community, various brotherhoods and numerous costumed groups play out well-known scenes from the Bible: from Adam and Eve in the Garden of Eden to the Passion of Christ. Next comes the story of Thierry of Alsace, Count of Flanders, who was awarded a few drops of the blood of Jesus by the patriarch of Jerusalem during the Second Crusade in 1146. This priceless relic was brought back to Bruges in a crystal bottle in 1150, since when believers have been able to revere the Holy Blood in the basilica of the same name. The final part of the procession is dedicated to the public veneration of the Holy Blood. Preceded by the Noble Fraternity of the Holy Blood, two prelates carry the reliquary through the city.

REIEFEEST - THE REIEN FESTIVAL: IN 2013 AS WELL!

From 16/8 to 24/8 a sound-and-light spectacular will once again be organized along the Reien – the city's canals – and on the Burg Square. Spectators will be effortlessly transported back to the fascinating days of the Middle Ages, the golden age of Burgundy, the flowering of the Renaissance and the frivolousness of the Baroque. More than 500 musicians, singers, dancers and actors will play out vivid tableaux vivants at a dozen or so different locations. These re-enacted scenes from history are performed repeatedly and independently of each other, so that visitors can set their own pace for completing the festival trajectory. From 9.00 p.m. to midnight. **INFORMATION** > www.brugge.be

July

Cactus Festival

An atmospheric open-air music festival, which offers a cocktail of rock, reggae, world music and dance.

INFORMATION > www.cactusfestival.be

Brugge Tripel Dagen (Bruges Triple Days)

Three days of free musical fun and entertainment, with well-known Flemish stars and 'Vlaanderen Zingt' (Flanders Sings), a sing-along happening for the general public.

INFORMATION >
www.bruggetripeldagen.be

'Klinkers'

Three weeks of free concerts at unforgettable locations in Bruges city centre.

INFORMATION > www.klinkers-brugge.be

August

Zandfeesten (Zand Festival)

Antiques and bric-a-brac market on 't Zand *(see above)*.

MAfestival

Each year this highly respected festival of ancient music – MA stands for Musica Antiqua – continues to attract the world's top performers to Bruges and Lissewege.

INFORMATION > tel. +32 (0)50 33 22 83, www.mafestival.be

Lichtfeest (Festival of Light)

Lissewege, the white village, lights up the night with pyrotechnic displays, atmospheric music and thousands of candles.

September

Open Monumentendag (Open Monument Day)

In 2013 many of Flanders' greatest historical monuments will open their doors to the general public for the 25th successive year. This jubilee celebration will be a 'best of' edition. INFORMATION > www.openmonumenten.be

'Kroenkelen' and Car-free Sunday

Wander through the green belt around Bruges by bike or on foot, or stroll through the quiet streets of the city on car-free Sunday (10.00 a.m.-6.00 p.m.).

Zandfeesten (Zand Festival)

Antiques and bric-a-brac market on 't Zand *(see above)*.

October

Jazz Brugge

A four-day festival of top-quality jazz concerts and jam sessions by some of Europe's leading musicians. Jazz Bruges is only organized once every two years. The next edition is in 2014.
INFORMATION > www.jazzbrugge.be

Razor Reel Fantastic Film Festival

Two weeks of fantastic fun for the lovers of fantastic films: from fairylike fantasies to hideous horror – and not just new releases, but also classic 'oldies' and cult masterpieces. In addition to the film showings, there are also workshops, exhibitions and a film & book fair.
INFORMATION > www.rrffff.be

November

Razor Reel Fantastic Film Festival

A festival for fantastic film fans *(see above)*.

Brugges Festival

Numerous concerts and performances explore a wide range of musical styles from around the world. Most of the concerts are held in the open air, although some (for example, if the weather is bad) take place in the City Theatre.
INFO: www.brugges-festival.be

December

Christmas Market and ice-rink

For a whole month you can soak up the Christmas atmosphere at various locations in the city (Markt, Simon Stevinplein and Walplein). On the Markt (Market Square) you can even pull on your ice-skates and glide gracefully around the temporary rink in the shadow of the Belfry.

December Dance

A festival of contemporary dance that allows many of today's leading choreographers to strut their stuff and do their thing!
INFORMATION > www.decemberdance.be

Take advantage!

With the Brugge City Card you can enjoy reduced admission to a wide number of events. You'll find all details in the free magazine events@brugge. (For further information, see page 12.)

Tips from Bruges connoisseurs

Working with the best view over Bruges, World Heritage City

Baroque In The Air

Frank Deleu, mad about music, knew how to make use of his passion. He is Bruges' carillonneur and he was a producer at Klara, the classical radio broadcasting station. As he is also an enthusiastic bon vivant who likes to wander through the city and her glorious past, it is abundantly clear that he is a unique personality who knows everything about Bruges' immaterial heritage and the history of her most famous tower.

IDENTIKIT

Name: Frank Deleu
Nationality: Belgian
Date of birth: 23 August 1952
He has lived in Bruges since 1984
The city's carilloneur, the man with the loftiest place
of work in the historic city centre

Frank Deleu looks down on Bruges; literally, that is. At least three times a week, the city's carillonneur climbs the three hundred and sixty-six steps of the belfry to reach his place of work. A long, 'uphill' walk that takes him eight minutes (providing visitors don't hold him up) and eventually brings him to one of the finest pieces of protected heritage in all Bruges. The 47 bells date mainly from the 18th century and have recently been restored. But in spite of his lonely place of work, the city bell-ringer is anything but a loner. 'It's just part and parcel of my job to play an instrument high and dry above the crowds. I don't do it for the applause, of course, I wouldn't hear it anyway. It's more of a passion that has grown on me.'

This iconic building – in medieval Flanders the belfries were regarded as a symbol of civic liberty – may have lost its original function of telling local people the time, but the carillon remains immensely popular with natives and visitors alike. In summer the evening recitals attract large crowds to the belfry's courtyard. Others prefer to listen to the sound of the bells at their own favourite spots in the city. The narrow Breidelstraat is one such spot, with its near-perfect acoustics, while listeners on the Burg also sitting on the front row, musically speaking!

Many writers have also sung the praises of the carillon of Bruges. Some of them were world-famous, such as Henry Wadsworth Longfellow, Charles Baudelaire and Jules Verne. *Le carilloneur de Bruges* even inspired three operas. And during the mid-19th century many English visitors came especially to Bruges, then the poorest city in the country, just to listen to the bells.

'Klankentoren'

Each day Frank Deleu is filled with admiration for the beauty that Bruges has

'Not only has Bruges been perfectly preserved in time, the streets are also kept very tidy.'

managed to preserve, the concentration of her museums and art works, her many intimate historical places and her busy cultural agenda. 'Not only has Bruges been perfectly preserved in time, the streets are also kept very tidy. I therefore hope that the city will be able to look after her historical face in the future, Like many of the Italian cities have done: by restricting traffic and rejecting contemporary architectural experiments. There is plenty of room for them away from the city centre.'

VIA BRUGENSIS

History is literally to be found on the cobbles of Bruges' streets, that is to say along the forty scallops that form the Bruges section of the Via Brugensis – the ancient pilgrims' route to Santiago de Compostela. The scallops are a modest homage to the thousands of pilgrims that have followed the route from the region of the Zwin via Bruges, Menin and Tournai to Sebourg near Valenciennes in the north of France, where they used to join the GR long-distance footpath.

SUMMERY CARILLON SOUNDS

The visitor who wishes to listen to Frank Deleu from the most advantageous spot should repair to the courtyard of the Belfry on a Monday or Wednesday evening during the summer months. The recital kicks off at 9.00 p.m. For the next hour the carilloneur will then indulge in his passion for his unique instrument. Deleu also plays the carillon throughout the year from 11.00 to 12.00 a.m. on Wednesday, Saturday and Sunday.

But this does not mean that the city bell-ringer is against innovation and modernity. For example, he is very enthusiastic about the Sound Factory, an interactive space for aural art on the panoramic roof of the Concertgebouw (Concert Hall). To celebrate 500 years of the carilloneur's art an inventory was made of all the bells in the historic city centre. The name of the maker and the place of manufacture were established for each bell, following which its own unique sound was recorded. Via two interactive touch screens, visitors can use these sounds to compose their own carillon concert and then listen to it being played over the city. See page 89 for all practical information on the Sound Factory.

Frank Deleu
best addresses

FAVOURITE SPOT IN TOWN

» **Onze-Lieve-Vrouw-ter-Potterie,**
   Potterierei 79,
   www.museabrugge.be

'The most moving place in town is the museum and church of Our Lady of the Pottery, a slightly out-of-the way spot, but one that well rewards the effort of finding it. The building is filled to the brim with jewels from a bygone age, from 16th-century household goods to furniture and unique paintings that time seems to have forgotten. An experience that will live long in your memory.'

RESTAURANTS

» **Diligence,** Hoogstraat 5,
   tel. +32 (0)50 33 16 60

'I am a big fan of the simple and authentic spontaneity of the Diligence. No matter who walks in through the door, the welcome is always warm and friendly, and they are immediately shown to a cosy table in this somewhat dark but always hospitable restaurant. No unnecessary fuss and frills. Just plain and simple Flemish dishes that will leave you wanting more.'

» **Restaurant Pergola,** Meestraat 7, tel. +32 (0)50 44 76 50,
   closed on Tuesday and Wednesday, www.restaurantpergola.be

'Bruges has many delightful terraces, but the terrace at Restaurant Pergola certainly comes in the top ten. Here, far from the noise of the crowds, you can admire the solemn beauty of the Groenerei, while sampling one of the restaurant's excellent and inventive dishes. Satisfaction guaranteed!'

» **Sint-Joris**, Markt 29, tel. +32 (0)50 33 30 62, www.restaurant-sintjoris.be

'Some people love top-quality gastronomic fireworks, but I prefer simple and tasty cooking. Such as the delicious everyday dishes you can find in the St. Joris. Its convenient and picturesque location on the Market Square makes it worth the recommendation alone!'

» **Carlito's**, Hoogstraat 21, tel. +32 (0)50 49 00 75, no closing day, www.carlitos.be

'Nothing is simpler yet more delicious than a really good pizza. Not too much topping, but just the right amount of day-fresh ingredients. Carlo also makes plenty of great-tasting pasta dishes, but I always go for one of those perfect pizzas. The simple things in life are often the best. Basta!'

» **Trium**, Academiestraat 23, tel. +32 (0)50 33 30 60, closed on Monday, www.trattoriatrium.be

'Every visit to Trium is a real experience. As soon as you enter, you think you are in Naples. Complete with gesticulating Italian waiters, who demonstrate all the flare and passion for which their native country is famous! Trium guarantees atmosphere and theatricality by the bucketful, which perfectly complements their honest and authentic pasta.'

CAFÉS

» **Craenenburg**, Markt 16, tel. +32 (0)50 33 34 02, www.craenenburg.be

'Craenenburg is the last "real" café on the Market Square. It was from this building that Margaret of York followed the great tournament of 1468. And it was also from here that Maximilian of Austria was forced to watch the torture and execution of his own sheriff and counsellor. Today, it is a favourite spot for local people, where they can catch up on all the latest city gossip and news.'

» **Concertgebouwcafé**, 't Zand 34, tel. +32 (0)50 47 69 81, closed on Sunday, Monday and Tuesday, www.concertgebouw.be/café

'The Concertgebouwcafé (at the Concert Hall) is the ideal place to enjoy an after-performance drink and chat. This trendy bar has real star-quality! Enjoy a coffee or some of their great finger food, as you watch the rest of the world pass by outside.'

» **Cultuurcafé Biekorf**, Naaldenstraat 4, closed on Sunday, www.ccbrugge.be

'You can find this café on the inner courtyard between the city's cultural centre and the library. It can be reached via both these buildings, and also from the Naaldenstraat. Why not give it a try? If you're lucky, you might drop in on one of their regular surprise acts.'

» **'t Hof van Rembrandt**, Eiermarkt 10, tel. +32 (0)50 33 74 50, www.thofvanrembrandt.be

''t Hof van Rembrandt is the 'place to be' for real beer-lovers. The café offers a wide selection of the finest beers in Belgium. In summer, you can enjoy the pleasant outdoor terrace. In winter, you can sip your pint next to the comfort of a blazing open hearth.'

» **'t Klein Venetië**, Braambergstraat 1, tel. +32 (0)50 33 10 37

''t Klein Venetië well deserves its name. The café has magnificent views of the city's canals and the Rozenhoedkaai. This is one of the most photographed locations in Bruges – so remember to smile!'

SHOPPING LIST

» **Rombaux**, Mallebergplaats 13, tel. +32 (0)50 33 25 75, closed on Sunday and Monday morning, www.rombaux.be

'This jam-packed music temple has been promoting classical music, jazz and top-quality contemporary music in Bruges for three generations. In all that time, the interior has hardly changed, apart from an occasional lick of paint. There is no better place to seek expert advice about really good music.'

» **Raaklijn**, Kuipersstraat 1, tel. +32 (0)50 33 67 20, closed on Sunday, www.boekhandelraaklijn.be

'The Raaklijn Book Store is a home from home for literature fans. It's a place where you can nose around for hours, just enjoying the pleasure of looking for what you want. And usually you will find something to tickle your fancy! You will often find me here.'

» **Callebert**, Wollestraat 25, tel. +32 (0)50 33 50 61, closed on Sunday and Monday morning, www.callebert.be

'A design-lover like me can always find something of interest at Callebert's. Iittala glass work, Alessi gadgets, Georg Jensen cutlery, a Stelton wine cooler, a bright pink pouffe from Quinze&Milan or a streamlined chair from Verner Panton: Callebert's has it all – and much more besides! Sometimes I hardly know where to start.'

» **Aenigma Antiquariaat**, Academiestraat 12, tel. +32 (0)50 37 17 25

'If I am looking for something rare or special, I always go and take a peek in Aenigma Antiques. With a little bit of luck, I can usually find something connected with the Belfry – my place of work – or with the history of the Bruges carillon.'

» **Cursief**, Baron Ruzettelaan 193, tel. +32 (0)50 35 39 25

'I am not really a great shopper, but if I am looking for old books or second-hand records I like to pop in to Cursief.'

SECRET TIP

» **Concertgebouw**,
   't Zand, tel. +32 (0)50 47 69 99

'Every year the Concertgebouw (Concert Hall) manages to charm friend and foe alike with its varied programme of the very highest quality. I am particularly looking forward to the annual Bach Academy at the end of January and the Gruuthuse project in April, as well as the dozens of other concerts that take place throughout the year. What's more, a visit to the Sound Factory is always great fun, because it allows you to be creative with different noises and sounds. You can experiment as much as you like.'

Flemish Primitives in the spotlight

Till-Holger Borchert sees respect as the key to success

He was born in Hamburg, he lives in Brussels and he thoroughly enjoys his work in Bruges as he finds himself surrounded by six centuries of fine arts, and especially the magnificent masterpieces of the Flemish Primitives. In 2002, Till-Holger Borchert was one of the curators of Bruges, Cultural Capital of Europe. Today he is chief curator of the Groeninge Museum and the Arentshuis.

IDENTIKIT

Name: Till-Holger Borchert
Nationality: German
Date of Birth: 4 January 1967
This chief curator of the Groeninge Museum is born in
Hamburg and lives in Bruges. He is also the author of
countless publications on the Flemish Primitives.

'Bruges is an exceptionally beautiful city,' says Till-Holger Borchert. 'What's more, It is also a wonderfully liveable place, partly because of the clever and careful way in which the city has been able to mix her medieval character with a modern ambiance. As early as the 13th century, the concentration of wealthy citizens enabled Bruges to become the commercial heart of North-western Europe. In the 15th century, the Burgundian authorities took successful structural measures which resulted in an increase of the population and had a positive effect on the city's further development. Just as importantly, Bruges was spared of the any ravages of the so-called Iconoclastic Fury, which caused so much damage in other cities. That spirit of respect and tolerance still pervades the city today. I must say it is a great joy to be here. The countless locals and visitors will surely fully agree with me.'

Madonnas from Around the Corner

'Nearly every day I go and greet two masterpieces: Jan van Eyck's *Madonna with*

'Nearly every day I go and greet two masterpieces.'

Canon Joris van der Paele at the Groeninge Museum and Hans Memling's *Madonna and Maarten van Nieuwenhove* at the Saint John's Hospital. I am not saying that I discover something new every time I look at them, but my curiosity and my

pleasure remain as great as ever. And I still try and find out new things about them. They just continue to fascinate me! I sometimes wonder why people from all corners of the world have always found the Flemish Primitives so absorbing. The answer perhaps lies in the fact that for the very first time in art history we are confronted with recognisable people and familiar objects that correspond to today's reality. Even a Madonna seems to look like the woman from around the corner. The Flemish Primitives laid the foundation of an artistic concept that in its realism is perfectly recognisable and therefore understandable to a modern-day observer. The Flemish Primitives discovered the individual. Quite a feat. Those Flemish painters were also dab hands at solving the problems. They explored space in an incredibly skilful and sophisti-

INTERESTING TOMBS

'The tomb of Charles the Bold isn't the only attraction of the Church of Our Lady. Mary of Burgundy, Charles' daughter and only child, lies buried in its crypt. She was barely twenty-five years old when she died after falling from her horse when hawking. The face on her coffin was modelled after her death mask. The metal casket with the heart of her son Philip the Fair is exhibited in the choir aisle.'

📷 MUSEUM SHOP

'Whoever enters the museum shop of the Groeninge Museum will leave with some wonderful memories, that I can assure you. Perhaps you will take home your favourite art treasures in that handsomely illustrated book or as a reproduction on a poster maybe, or depicted on a few picture postcards. And why don't you surprise yourself with an original souvenir? I have caught not only some of my delighted fellow curators buying just such a present for themselves, but my wife as well!'

cated way, for example by placing a mirror somewhere in the room. In Memling's diptych, a round mirror on the left-hand side behind the Madonna reflects the interior she is sitting in. In it, her own silhouette is painted just a whisker away from the silhouette of the patrician Maarten van Nieuwenhove, Memling's patron. Truly magnificent. Are these works of art still capable of moving me?

Absolutely. For pure emotion a painter like Rogier van der Weyden touches me more deeply than Jan van Eyck. The works of Van Eyck or Memling impress me more with their intellectual and conceptual qualities. Van der Weyden and Van Eyck: it is worth visiting the treasure houses of Bruges, even if only for the pleasure of enjoying these two opposite ends of artistic spectrum.'

Till-Holger Borchert
best addresses

FAVOURITE SPOT

'The great churches of Bruges possess wonderful art collections, containing pieces that wouldn't disgrace any topflight museum. Don't forget to look up at the tower of the Church of Our Lady. It is, with its 122 metres, the second tallest brick building in the world. When in Saint Saviour's, do go and marvel at the frescoes in the baptistery. And Saint James' Church is worth its while for the impressive **mausoleum of the De Gros family**, because this sculptural masterpiece reveals par excellence the self-confidence and power of the Burgundian elite.'

RESTAURANTS

» **Den Amand**, Sint-Amandsstraat 4,
tel. +32 (0)50 34 01 22,
closed on Sunday and Wednesday,
www.denamand.be

'In Den Amand I once saw a German restaurant critic copy out the entire menu card. You can't get higher praise than that! A small and elegant bistro, where you will find both tourists and local people enjoying the excellent food.'

» **Rock Fort**, Langestraat 15, tel. +32 (0)50 34 41 13, www.rock-fort.be
'Rock Fort serves original, contemporary dishes with a modern twist. It's cooking is so good that the place is packed all week long. Local people love it, and I also like to pop

in from time to time. But be careful: it is closed during the weekends.'

» **'t Schrijverke**, Gruuthusestraat 4, tel. +32 (0)50 33 29 08,
   closed on Monday, www.tschrijverke.be

'This homely restaurant is named after a poem by Guido Gezelle, which hangs in a place of honour next to the door. But 't Schrijverke is above all rightly famed for its delicious regional dishes and its "Karmeliet" beer on tap.'

» **Tanuki**, Oude Gentweg 1, tel. +32 (0)50 34 75 12, www.tanuki.be

'A little piece of Japan in the heart of Bruges. A true temple of food, where you immediately drop your voice to the level of a whisper, so that you don't disturb the silent enjoyment of the other diners. In the open kitchen the chef does magical things with sushi and sashimi, and prepares his seven course menus with true oriental serenity.'

» **Den Gouden Harynck**, Groeninge 25, tel. +32 (0)50 33 76 37,
   closed on Sunday and Monday, www.dengoudenharynck.be

'Den Gouden Harynck is a household name in Bruges, known and loved by foodies of all kinds. It is also one of the most pleasant star-rated restaurants in the city - as anyone who has ever been there will tell you.'

CAFÉS

» **Boru Irish Bar & Restaurant**,
   Burg 8, tel. +32 (0)50 34 91 45,
   www.boru.be

'It's always party time in this Irish pub, with its distinctive international atmosphere. Boru is the kind of place where you can rub shoulders with the whole world at the bar.'

» **The Druid's Cellar**, Sint-Amandsstraat 11, tel. +32 (0)50 61 41 44,
   www.thedruidscellar.eu

'I like to drop in at The Druid's Cellar every now and again, even if only to watch Drew, my favorite barkeeper, in action. Or simply to relax and enjoy a glass from their wide range of Scottish and Irish whiskies. They always taste just that little bit better in The Druids.'

» **Du Phare**, Sasplein 2, tel. +32 (0)50 34 35 90, closed on Tuesday, www.duphare.be

'The terrace at Du Phare is highly recommended, and on cold days there is even outdoor heating. Indoors there is the pleasing blues atmosphere of a typical 'brown' café. This is a place where they serve the better kind of bistro cooking. An address that is particularly popular with locals.'

» **Den Express**, Stationsplein

'The Den Express station bar is ideal for people like me, who travel a lot. Here I can enjoy a quiet coffee before setting off on my journey, safe from all the hustle and bustle going on outside.'

» **Hollandse Vismijn**, Vismarkt 4, closed on Tuesday, tel. +32 (0)50 33 33 01

'Whenever I fancy one of the popular Belgian beers, you will probably find me in the Hollandse Vismijn. This cheap and cheerful 'people's pub' is on the Fish Market. It is the type of café where everybody knows everybody and where you always get a warm welcome. Cheers!'

SHOPPING LIST

» **De Striep**, Katelijnestraat 42, closed on Sunday morning and Monday morning, www.striepclub.be

'For modern comic strips I always head straight for De Striep. There you will find all the most recent titles, as well as a fine selection of special editions and collector's items. A place where young and old alike can spend hour after happy hour!'

» **Deldycke Delicatessen**, Wollestraat 23, tel. +32 (0)50 33 43 35, closed on Tuesday, www.deldycke.be

'In the 15th century the Spaniard Pedro Tafur was already praising Bruges for its wide available selection of exotic fruits and rare spices. The Deldycke Delicatessen is proud to continue this centuries-old tradition. Here, all your culinary wishes will be fulfilled.'

» **Kleding Parallax**, Zuidzandstraat 17, closed on Sunday, www.parallax.be

'I always buy my socks at Parallax, but they are also experts at stylishly camouflaging my beer belly! Highly recommended for other fashion victims and the vestimentally challenged! Boss, Scabal, Zilton, Falke: you can find them all here.'

» **Antiquariaat Van de Wiele**, Sint-Salvatorskerkhof 7, closed on Tuesday, Wednesday and Sunday, www.marcvandewiele.com

'For art and history I was fortunate enough to discover Marc Van de Wiele Antiques. This is undoubtedly one of the best addresses in a city that is rich in antique shops. The place to find unique, illustrated books from days long gone by.'

» **Boekhandel De Reyghere**, Markt 12, closed on Sunday, www.dereyghere.be

'For all my other reading material I rely on De Reyghere, conveniently located on the Market Square. Foreign visitors feel instantly at home in this book and newspaper store, primarily because of the large number of international titles it has on sale.'

SECRET TIP

» **Museumshop**, Arentshof, Dijver 16, closed on Monday, www.museabrugge.be

» **Folklore Museum, Gezelle Museum, Our Lady of the Pottery, Jerusalem Chapel** and **Lace Centre**: info on pages 81-82

'Whenever I want to take a breather, I saunter down Saint Anne's, Bruges' most striking working-class neighbourhood. You can still sense the charm of an authentic community in the streets around the Folklore Museum. It goes without saying that it is very peaceful there at night, a very rare occurrence in a city like Bruges. The area boasts many fascinating places, too. Off the cuff, if I may: Our Lady of the Pottery, the Lace Centre, medieval **Jerusalem Chapel** and the Gezelle Museum.'

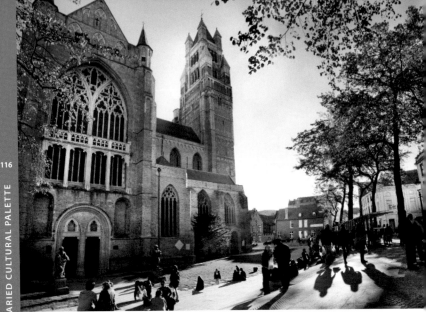

A varied cultural palette

Brody Neuenschwander, an American in Bruges

Looking back it seemed almost inevitable that the world-famous calligrapher, Brody Neuenschwander, would one day end up in Bruges. It was his love for the Flemish Primitives (and his wife, of course!) that first pushed him in this direction. His medieval house, with its 14th century mural paintings, will ensure that he now stays for good. The story of a Texan with a Bruges heart.

IDENTIKIT

Name: Brody Neuenschwander
Nationality: American
Date of Birth: 8 September 1958

Has been living in Bruges since 1993. World-renowned calligraphist, whose important commissions include work for the American, British and Belgian governments, as well as the BBC and the Royal Mail; a man who stands with one foot in the medieval past of Bruges and the other foot firmly in the future.

A VARIED CULTURAL PALETTE

Brody Neuenschwander might well have been born and bred in the wide open spaces of Houston, Texas, but he has always belonged in Bruges. He was a part of the city and the city was a part of him. When, as an art student in distant America, he first learnt about the Flemish Primitives, he immediately jumped on a plane and came to see for himself. And he was impressed by what he found. 'I was just 20. I stood on the Bonifacius Bridge and looked around me: "Wow!" I thought, "this is a really great city". At that time, he never dreamed that he might one day live here. The years passed. Brody studied many of the medieval breviaries produced in Bruges, perhaps the city's most important 'export product' during the glory years of the Middle Ages. When his grandmother gave him a substantial sum of money, he immediately went out and bought one of his own. 'This was my own little piece of medieval treasure, a thing of rare beauty.' It was only later in London that he first met his wife-to-be – a local girl from Bruges. It was clear from the start that the

'I stood on the Bonifacius Bridge and looked around me: "Wow!" I thought, "this is a really great city".'

newly married couple would make their home in her native city. So the breviary was sold and exchanged for a beautiful house fronting onto one of the city's many canals. It later transpired that this was the oldest house in what had once been the medieval harbour quarter. While he was renovating one of the rooms, the do-it-yourselver suddenly cried out in amazement. 'At first, my wife thought that I had fallen off the ladder, but in fact I had discovered a medieval mural painting, hidden way for centuries beneath layers of plaster and paint. And it wasn't just a rough design sketch but a completed work, which now ranks as one of the most important wall paintings of its kind in Flanders.' But Brody keeps a sense of perspective. 'I guess I just exchanged one work of art for another. And yes, it's fun to think that I was somehow destined to live here, in this house.'

Bruges: the world centre for Western calligraphy

Although the world-famous calligrapher could now live anywhere in the world he wants to, he remains faithful to his adopted home town. 'Here, there is a new treat for your eyes, almost every day of the year. And no matter where you go and what you see, it is always better in Bruges. What's more, the city is now the centre of Western calligraphy. There is no other place in Europe or America that even comes close. Bruges not only has a great number of professional calligraphists, but also several calligraphy shops and a wide range of calligraphy courses. And we are

GENETIC HERITAGE

'Texas is a land of wide open spaces. Everything is big. The houses, the landscape, the restaurant tables… Here, the scale of everything is different. In Bruges you only have to dig a hole in your back garden to stumble across the past. First a tile, then a bit of sand, then another tile, next a brick… The different layers of history run so deep and are so close together that things evolve more slowly here. An American will sometimes change his mind overnight. Someone from Bruges will not.'

GRUUTHUSE MANUSCRIPT IS THE 'STAR' IN THE 'LOVE & DEVOTION' EXPO

Bruges circa 1400. An unknown patron commissions a number of copyists to collect and transcribe a selection of poems, prayers and songs. And so the Gruuthuse manuscript was born. Even today, this manuscript – made in Bruges – offers us a wealth of useful information about Middle Dutch literature and is a crucial source for the study of culture and history in the Low Countries during the Late Middle Ages. For many centuries, this parchment book remained in private ownership, until it was purchased in 2007 by the Royal Library in The Hague. Via the link http://www.kb.nl/bladerboeken/het-gruuthuse-handschrift van de Koninklijke Bibliotheek, you can leaf your way (virtually) through the pages of the manuscript. Highly recommended!

In 2013 the Gruuthuse manuscript will briefly be 'coming home' for a unique exhibition that will catapult you straight back into the golden age of medieval Bruges. An exhibition in which you will also be able to admire Brody Neuenschwander's handiwork.

From 22 March to 23 June 2013, Gruuthuse Museum, daily from 9.30 a.m. to 5.00 p.m., closed on Monday.

not standing still. We are constantly active, seeking to bring the past and the present together in new creative ways. In Bruges, innovation always stimulates some kind of dialogue with the past, and that is what I find so interesting. The unique exhibition with the Gruuthuse Manuscript (see above) is perhaps the best example of what I mean.'

If an artist elsewhere in the world or one of Neuenschwander's important 'customers' (the American, British and Belgian governments, the BBC, etc.) need a top-quality calligrapher, they just pick up the phone and call Brody. One week he will be working for director Peter Greenaway, the next week on a documentary series for the BBC, and the week after that on some project of his own. Sitting still – and doing nothing – is not an option.

Brody Neuenschwander
best addresses

FAVOURITE SPOT

» **The attics of the Sint-Janshospi-
   taal (St. John's Hospital),**
   Mariastraat 38

'In these attics, you can hear and feel the
silence. It is as if time has stood still. With
the huge beams, massive wooden pillars
and the Burgundian tiled floor, it is easy to
imagine yourself back in the 14th century.'

RESTAURANTS

» **Books and Brunch**, Garenmarkt 30,
   tel. +32 (0)50 70 90 79,
   www.booksandbrunch.be

'Books and Brunch is a unique and very
welcome addition to the food scene in
Bruges. A delightful breakfast, coffee and
lunch address, where you can pick up a
book or two, or simply enjoy a good read
while you are waiting for your delicious
homemade cake or perfect cappuccino. And the kids will also find something to
keep them amused in the mini-library.'

» **De Lotus**, Wapenmakersstraat 5, tel. +32 (0)50 33 10 78,
   www.lotus-brugge.be

'This vegetarian lunch restaurant is now a Bruges classic. For the past 20 years it has
been offering tasty vegetarian dishes in its sober yet refined décor. Simple wooden
stools and chairs, and everything served on their attractive ceramic tableware. Solo-
eaters can flick through one of the many available papers and magazines.'

» **Lieven**, Philipstockstraat 45, tel. +32 (0)50 68 09 75, www.etenbijlieven.be
'In just a short time the stylish Lieven has grown into a trendy success restaurant. The menu is limited: just four starters and four main courses. But the food is exceptionally refined, in a contemporary interior with character.'

» **A'Qi**, Gistelse Steenweg 686, 8200 Sint-Andries, tel. +32 (0)50 30 05 99, www.restaurantaqi.be
'A'Qi means something like 'life force' and that is exactly what this quality restaurant wants to offer. Each new visit is a total experience that nourishes both body and mind. Based on the classic traditions of Flemish cooking, but enriched with flashes of foreign inspiration.'

» **Cafedraal**, Zilverstraat 38, tel. +32 (0)50 34 08 45, www.cafedraal.be
'This 15th century building has an enchanting enclosed garden, which you can enjoy from the first sun of spring until deep into the autumn. The specialities of the house are the classic meat and fish dishes for which Flanders is famous.'

CAFÉS

» **One**, Arsenaalstraat 55,
   tel. +32 (0)50 33 80 88,
   www.one-minnewater.be

'One of the most beautiful terraces in Bruges, hidden away in one of the city's most romantic parks. The ideal place to enjoy a quiet aperitif, some tapas or a coffee and a cake. And all in an elegant setting that cheers the heart and pleases the eye.'

» **De Garre**, De Garre 1, tel. +32 (0)50 34 10 29, www.degarre.be
'You can find this authentic 'beer' cafe in one of the smallest streets in Bruges. Here you can choose from no fewer than 130 different beers, ranging from regional brews and commercial beers on tap to bottled abbey ales. Some are well-known, some are not so well-known – but they are all well worth a try. Cheers!'

» **Bar of the Grand Hotel Casselbergh**, Hoogstraat 6, tel. +32 (0)50 44 65 00, www.grandhotelcasselbergh.com
'This glorious four-star hotel has a bar that is as magnificent as it is charming. High ceilings, luxurious wall hangings, dazzling chandeliers, open hearths and a wide selection of quality drinks, with *premium brands* from both home and abroad.'

SHOPPING LIST

» **Symposion**, Oostmeers 41, tel. +32 (0)50 33 61 31, www.symposion.be

'A writer's paradise, where calligraphic soul-mates can commune with each other. Here you can not only find everything a calligrapher needs, but there is also a quiet place to read and a fine section of carefully crafted gifts and knick-knacks. From calligraphed kitchen aprons through framed silk-screen prints to modest but original postcards.'

» **Atelier Maud Bekaert**, Sint-Clarastraat 40, tel. +32 (0)475 26 95 58, www.lettersinsteen.be
'It was poetry that first led Maud Bekaert to take up the art of letter-cutting. Today she engraves her own poetry in letters of stone and several of her creations can be seen here and there in the streets of Bruges. Her small but atmospheric workshop is the place for souvenirs with character.'

» **simBOLik**, Katelijnestraat 139 , tel. +32 (0)495 30 70 56, www.simbolik.be
'Calligraphers can enjoy themselves to their hearts content every Thursday, Friday and Saturday in this open workshop. And every first Sunday of the month a poet, theatre-maker or musician is invited to come and 'do his creative thing'. In short, a place where creative souls can come into contact with each other in comfortable and informal surroundings.'

» **De Kringloopwinkel**, Langestraat 169-171, tel. +32 (0)50 34 94 00, www.klctrad.be

'This is where true creativity begins. For next to nothing you can pick up all kinds of interesting things in this second-hand store. Some are just useful; others might be a source of artistic inspiration. Who knows? From vintage handbags through porcelain objects to full dinner services! Well worth a look.'

» **De Andere Kijk**, Garenmarkt 28, tel. +32 (0)50 34 21 61

'*You name it, we frame it* is the slogan of this workshop, where you can indeed frame all your artistic and other treasures, whatever their shape and size.'

SECRET TIP

» **The Sint-Gillis district**

'A popular, working-class area, with street after street of small workers' houses, dominated by a magnificent church and the memory of a mysterious cemetery, now long since disappeared, where (amongst others) Hans Memling was buried. That, in a nutshell, is the St. Giles' Quarter. This was, indeed, the place where Memling lived and worked. In 1480 he bought a house in the Sint-Jorisstraat and a few years later he also bought the adjoining property, 'Den Ingel'. Both buildings were demolished in the 19th century. There is now a plaque marking the site, which reminds people of the life and work of this great Flemish Primitive. There is a second such plaque in the St. Giles' Church, where he was buried in 1494. While you are searching to find these plaques, don't forget to admire the fine combination of the Gothic and Neo-Gothic styles in Sint-Gillis. In particular, the quarter offers an opportunity to stop and admire the often underrated qualities of the Neo-Gothic period. This was the last real crafts movement in Western architecture, which played a not insignificant role in shaping the Bruges that we can still see today.'

Bruges, the bike-friendly city

A city made for people, with beautiful surroundings

Marina Tasiopoulos was born in Sweden of Greek parentage. After various detours in London and Paris, she eventually found her way to Belgium, where she promptly fell in love with Jos from… Bruges. Today, this modern European lady is mum to a bouncing Bruges bambino and has lost her heart to cycling – and to her adopted native city.

IDENTIKIT

Name: Marina Tasiopoulos
Nationality: Swedish/Greek
Date of Birth: 12 July 1975
Has been living in Bruges since 2003.
Marina works for the EU.

Marina's Bruges story begins with her arrival in Brussels for a training course. During a weekend in Bruges, the Greek-Swedish Marina got to know Jos Teughels, who runs QuasiMundo Bike Tours. One thing led to another, so that Marina was soon back to learn more about the city and it wider surroundings, pedalling frantically in the bike-tracks of Jos.

In the meantime, Marina is no longer the tourist that she then was. But she still looks at the city through different eyes. 'I am still amazed every day by just how beautiful Bruges really is. I have seen many different places and I have lived in several of them. So I am in a good position to compare. And I know that Bruges is unique, truly unique. You simply have to be prepared to accept it for what it is. Most mornings I come quite early near the Beguinage and I never fail to be impressed by what I see. Sometimes I watch the sun rising over the tiled roofs, sometimes everything is shrouded in mist, with not a person in sight. And then

'I am still amazed every day by just how beautiful Bruges really is.'

BRUGES: A BIKER'S PARADISE

It is no coincidence that the Tour of Flanders – Flanders' most celebrated cycling race – starts each year on the Market Square in Bruges. Bruges is the biking city 'par excellence'. Not only do many of the local people make most of their short journeys by bike, but tourists also find it a great way to discover the city and its surroundings. You can hire bikes – standard models, tandems or even electrically-driven – at several different locations *(also see page 18: bicycle rental points)*. And once you have your wheels, you are ready to explore. Perhaps as part of a guided tour? Or maybe you prefer to cruise solo? It's up to you!

many of the world's larger metropolises. 'You can still say hello to your neighbour, or have a chat with your baker, or ask how the chemist's daughter is getting on at university. It is these simple things that make life in Bruges so appealing.'

Discover the Bruges' wet- and woodlands

Although Marina is a big fan of the 'vesten' – the network of moats and ramparts around Bruges – and although she and

there is the evening, when the city magically empties of tourists and day visitors around six o'clock. This is the moment when Bruges once again belongs to the local people, to the people who were born here and live here.'

This globetrotter appreciates that Bruges is a city made for people, a human city with a human face, so different from

GUIDED BICYCLE TOURS IN THE CITY AND SURROUNDINGS OF BRUGES

Whoever wants to explore Bruges and/or its surrounding wet- and woodlands by bike is well advised to get in touch with one or more of the following three organizations *(also see page 27)*. You can book an interesting guided tour with Jos Teughels, Marina's husband and the man behind QuasiMundo. You can choose between 'Bruges by bike' – a ride through the city itself – or 'Border by bike', which takes you through the pleasant countryside beyond the city walls.

The Pink Bear Bike Tours offers a tour to the delightful town of Damme. The four-hour route includes plenty of stops along the way, so that you can admire the scenery and sample various local specialities.

The Green Bike Tour/Sun Bike Tour also organizes guided trips through the polder landscape around Bruges, including a stop in the heart of historic Damme.

MAKE YOUR OWN CYCLE ROUTE

Bruges is circled by bike-friendly 'vesten' (ramparts), while the more adventurous, who wish to explore beyond the city limits, will find an extensive network of wide and gentle cycle paths to lead them through the pleasant countryside of the Bruges' wet- and woodlands.

There are no fewer than 12 signposted provincial routes that you can follow. There is also the 'Brugse Ommeland' Cycle Network (www.brugseommeland.be), which allows you to move between different numbered junction points, just as you please. For each route there is a folder available, complete with map and detailed route descriptions.

If you are looking for a little something extra, you may care to try one of the themed routes based on the junction points of the Brugse Ommeland Cycle Network. These include: 'Country estates – the summer retreats of the Bruges elite', 'Bruges swans and Damme geese – a bird-lovers biking route', 'Forts and dykes between Bruges and Damme', 'Biking from sweet water to salt water', and 'Biking to abbeys and castles in and around Bruges'. Once again, there is a folder for each route, with background information, details about sites of interest along the way and a handy fold-out map. The city's info offices [i] Markt (Historium), 't Zand (Concertgebouw) and Stationsplein (Station) can provide you with full information about the many different cycling possibilities!

her daughter have made it their mission to give the city's many child-friendly parks a real testing ('We regard ourselves as quality controllers'), what she really likes to do is to get out her bike and set course for the 'Brugse Ommeland' – the countryside that surrounds the city. 'As soon as you leave the city, your find yourself in a different world. A quiet, peaceful landscape of arrow-straight canals, open fields and trees. And all within a kilometre of the Market Square! It's unique, absolutely unique!' says Marina.

'Damme, Oostkerke, Lissewege: they are delightful little villages, each with its own charm and character, and all well worth a visit. Panoramic, unspoiled green sceneries – and all within a stone's throw of Bruges.'

Has Marina found her place in the world? 'With all the greenery in Bruges, all those parks and playgrounds, it's a really great place for a kid to grow up in. We are definitely not thinking of moving!'

Marina Tasiopoulos
best addresses

FAVOURITE SPOT

'The woods in Beisbroek and Tillegem are great places for walks, both summer and winter. Ideal for stretching your legs and clearing your mind! What's more, both domains have fun play areas for the kids. And if we want wide open vistas and fresh sea air, then there is nothing better than a stroll along **the beach at Zeebrugge**.'

RESTAURANTS

» **Sale e Pepe**, Kleine Sint-Amands-straat 1, tel. +32 (0)50 61 51 55
'Hidden away just behind the Market Square, this is (in my opinion, at least) the best place in town to experience pure and honest Italian cooking, prepared by a real Sicilian cook!'

» **Anurak Thai**, Moerkerkse Steenweg 57, Sint-Kruis, tel. + 32 (0)50 68 83 38, www.anurakthai.be
'You can find this authentic Thai restaurant just outside the Kruispoort (St. Cross Gate). Here you can eat real Thai cooking in a quiet and pleasant décor. Their *Penang Nua* is unbelievably good!'

» **The Olive Tree**, Wollestraat 3, tel. +32 (0)50 33 00 81, www.theolivetree-brugge.com

'An excellent Greek restaurant for food-lovers who are keen to avoid Zorba music and Acropolis look-alike interiors, but just want good, traditional home-made Greek dishes. Highly recommended.'

» **Pastis**, Speelmansrei 8, tel. +32 (0)50 34 18 09, www.pastis.be

'This pleasant bistro shines and sparkles on the Speelmansrei, one of the earliest defensive walls around medieval Bruges. Here you can eat pastas, salads or tapas, or else choose something from the monthly suggestions board, or perhaps even try the menu of the month. There is also plenty of choice for vegetarians.'

» **'t Bagientje**, Oostmeers 130, tel. +32 (0)50 33 11 20, www.bagientje.be

''t Bagientje has a charm that is difficult – if not impossible – to resist. It's like going to visit your old Flemish grandmother. A place where they serve classic Flemish cooking – and where you will never leave the table still feeling hungry!'

CAFÉS

» **Li O Lait**, Dweersstraat 30, tel. +32 (0)50 70 85 70, www.liolait.be

'This is a new coffee house, but it has plenty of old-world charm. A paradise for coffee-lovers, who know their filter-coffee from their espresso and their latte from their cappuccino. Tea-lovers will also find an impressive range of choice, while those with a sweet tooth can opt for a white hot chocolate. Trendsetters may prefer an ice-cold coffee shake, whereas the true hedonists will undoubtedly go for a refreshing glass of cava.'

» **L'Estaminet**, Park 5, tel. +32 (0)50 33 09 16, http://users.telenet.be/fclestaminet/lestaminet.htm

'A traditional 'brown' pub where local people – from dockers to doctors – and tourists have been coming for ages, to enjoy a friendly glass or two at the bar. They also serve a delicious, home-made spaghetti-gratin, which you can order until deep in the night.'

» **Café Rose Red**, Cordoeaniersstraat 16, tel. +32 (0)50 33 90 51,
www.cordoeanier.be/rosered

'Although in the middle of the city, this café, with its pleasant walled garden, is slightly hidden away. Rose Red specializes in abbey-brewed beers and they also serve a beer of the month. And if you have one too many, you can always book a room and sleep it off in the hotel next door.'

» **De Stoepa**, Oostmeers 124, tel. +32 (0)50 33 04 54, www.stoepa.be

'This meet-greet-and-eat pub is a real hot-spot. The impressive interior courtyard is the ideal place to enjoy a special 'jenever', an obscure rum, a fine wine or one of their wide range of cocktails. Always open till late, but sometimes difficult to find a place to sit – or even stand!'

» **Barazar**, Langestraat 40, tel. +32 (0)50 33 88 89, www.hotelflanders.com

'A chic hotel bar, famed for its cocktails, cava and champagne. Great in winter, when you can gather around the open hearth, but equally great in summer, when you can relax on the pleasant outdoor terrace. Stylish and sophisticated – and well worth a try.'

SHOPPING LIST

» **Chez Madame Moustache**,
Ezelstraat 16, tel. +32 (0)50 70 50 28,
www.chezmadamemoustache.be

'Two of my friends run this unusual concept store. Here you can find fine ceramics, vintage design, hand-made postcards, and heart-breakingly romantic paintings, but you can also treat yourself to a piping-hot espresso and a thick slice of cake. Yummy!'

» **Lunabloom**, Eekhoutstraat 17b, tel. +32 (0)50 34 75 09, www.lunabloom.be

'A concept store for happy kids. In Lunabloom you will only find fun things: for girls and boys, both young and not-so-young. A unique address, where everything rings true. One of those shops where every child wants everything – and they want it now!'

» **Mini-Me**, Kleine Sint-Amandsstraat 10, tel. +32 (0)50 68 05 24, www.mini-me.be
'This is the place for cool skater outfits for fashionable young boys and girls about town.
From shirts and sweaters, through baby-sneakers to hip hats for the very smallest.'

» **The Chocolate Line**, Simon Stevinplein 19, tel. +32 (0)50 34 10 90,
   www.thechocolateline.be
'If I have friends to visit, then I always buy in a good supply of chocolate. And I always
tell them the story of the shop's larger-than-life frontman, Dominique Persoone. He was
the man who taught the Rolling Stones to snort chocolate powder! When Ron Wood
and Charlie Watts were in Brussels to celebrate their birthday, Persoone introduced
them to the *Chocolate Shooter*.'

» **Galerie Pinsart**, Genthof 21, tel. +32 (0)50 67 50 66, www.pinsart.be
'The Genthof runs parallel to – and is slightly hidden behind – the Spiegelrei, but is a street
that in recent years has blossomed into new life. It now contains a number of interesting
shops and galleries. Such as Galerie Pinsart, for example, which has transformed an 18th
century mansion into a modern space for contemporary art. One of my favourites.'

SECRET TIP

» **Graaf Visartpark**
'My daughter and I are both big fans of this recently renovated park on the edge of
town. In particular, the well-thought-out playing area is great for kids, and guarantees hours of fun every time. We are often to be found here during the weekend.'

Bruges, culinary centre

Bob Eck, a New York foodie living for the day in Bruges

A New Yorker who swaps The Big Apple for the Market Square in Bruges: it sounds like it must be a joke – but that is precisely what Bob Eck, an international manager, did. In his search for a more relaxed style of life, he crossed the Atlantic and set up shop in Flanders. That his new home could satisfy his love for great food was just an added bonus. A conversation with a Dutch-speaking New Yorker.

IDENTIKIT

Name: Bob Eck
Nationality: American
Date of Birth: 3 June 1963
Born in Cincinnati, Ohio, USA
Has lived in Bruges since 2011 / Has been living in Bruges since 2011. Bob Eck is a self-employed marketing consultant and dedicated foodie.

For many years, Bob Eck led a hundred-mile-an-hour existence in the hustle and bustle of New York. He worked long days followed by long nights in the vibrant after-hours social scene of one of the world's greatest cities. It was only when he finally got back to his apartment – usually in the early hours of the morning – that he was able to relax and unwind. But he found himself dreaming increasingly of a different kind of existence, a more 'human' way of life. 'I wanted to live more and work less. I wanted balance. But I couldn't find it. I was still working much more than I was living. In fact, work was my life, it was all I was doing.'

WELCOME IN THE GASTRONOMIC MECCA OF EUROPE

'Even before we moved to Bruges, I already knew that you can eat here very well – very well indeed. There is no city in the world that has more Michelin stars per 100,000 inhabitants than Bruges.'

In the section 'Restaurants of distinction' you can read which local restaurants offer star-quality cooking, which ones have been awarded the Bib-Gourmand label and which ones can boast a nice score in the GaultMillau guide. They are numbers that will tickle the palette and the imagination of every hungry gourmet! *(See pages 30-33)*

The fact that he and his partner were unable to marry in New York – something they later did in Connecticut – simply strengthened his urge to leave. The pair decided to move home – not just to a new town or a new state, but to a new country – Belgium, 'a country that clearly promotes tolerance'. His eye immediately settled on the mondaine, worldly city of Bruges. 'Bruges is a beautiful city where you can relax and find peace with yourself. The quality of life is so much higher here than in New York, and thanks to the fantastic food and wine culture there is al-

A VALHALLA FOR FOODIES

'Nothing is so much fun as running your errands at the market. And in Bruges you can do that almost every day of the week. I always buy my fresh fish at the delightful old fish market. And I get my fruit, vegetables and flowers every Wednesday, when dozens of stalls take over the Market Square for the morning. Or on Saturday, when there are markets on both 't Zand and the Beursplein. And if I discover that I have forgotten something for the weekend, I can always nip down to the atmospheric Sunday market in Sint-Michiels. So there's choice enough!'

'Here people still take the time to cook properly;
and wherever you go it's just so easy to find really fantastic ingredients.'

ways plenty to enjoy. What's more, the pace of living is healthier in Bruges than in Manhattan. Here you have more time for your family, your friends and for good eating! This makes Bruges more relaxed, more open, friendlier. Here people still take the time to cook properly; and wherever you go it's just so easy to find really fantastic ingredients. All this means that, for me, Bruges is like a fairy-tale come true, a city that combines medieval charm with modern, high-tech comfort.'

Hours of dining fun

Even visiting a restaurant is more relaxed on this side of the ocean. 'In New York everything has to go fast. Each restaurant does two or three shifts each evening. Enjoying a nice chat after you meal is simply not done – they want you out as quickly as possible. In Bruges the focus is on what I call 'slow enjoyment'. You start your meal at around eight in the evening and it is only three or four hours later that you finally head for home. In this country, dining out is not only about what you get on your plate (although that's usually pretty-damned good); it's about the whole experience. Restaurateurs are not bothered about turning shift after shift; they are happy if they can send their customers home satisfied at the end of the evening. Because satisfied customers will keep on coming back for more. In my opinion, it's a much smarter approach.

I had expected to find a better quality of life in Flanders, but each day my expectations are surpassed – big time! I am thinking, for example, of all that wonderful Bruges chocolate. It's not without good reason that Bruges is rightly called the capital of chocolate. And as for all those top-quality beers, with the city's own beer, 'Brugse Zot', leading the way… Yep, life here is really great!'

A CELEBRATION OF FOOD AND DRINK

'The people of Bruges find it hard to disguise their Burgundian, bon-vivant past. A fact that is amply proven with events like *KookEet* (CookEat) and the Bruges Beer Festival. During *KookEet* the best chefs in Bruges serve delicious 'taster' menus all weekend long on the Market Square, while the Beer Festival allows you to sample all the many excellent brews for which Bruges and Belgium are famous. Two great events – highly recommended for every budding Burgundian!'
(You can find a detailed events calendar on the website http://events.brugge.be)

Bob Eck

best addresses

FAVOURITE SPOT

'There is a small park behind the **St. Saviour's Cathedral**: just a handful of benches and a small plot of grass, where I regularly stop for a break. You are always sitting in the sun and you have a magnificent view of a mighty oak tree. It is surprisingly quiet: a mini-escape in the middle of town.'

RESTAURANTS

» **Chez Olivier**, Meestraat 9,
   tel. +32 (0)50 33 36 59,
   www.chezolivier.be

'If you have something to celebrate or are willing to splash out a little bit more, Chez Olivier is the perfect address. The food is better than good and the location is enchanting, with a view over the Canals. An unforgettable evening is guaranteed!'

» **Quatre Mains**, Philipstockstraat 8, tel. +32 (0)50 33 56 50, www.4mains.com
'The food here is really great and you can decide the size of your own portions. From tapas right through to your main course and dessert. And the couple that run the place, Leen and Olivier, are just as fantastic as the food they serve.'

» **Tom's Diner**, West-Gistelhof 23, tel. +32 (0)50 33 33 82, www.tomsdiner.be
'Although this restaurant was recently renovated by a famous interior designer, it still has a delightfully casual atmosphere. Heart-warming. Here you can eat Belgian dishes with an international twist, but without paying a fortune.'

» **Merveilleux**, Muntpoort 8, tel. +32 (0)50 61 02 09, www.merveilleux.eu
'A hidden jewel, where you can go for a slice of cake, a special tea, a deliciously aromatic coffee or a surprising lunch. Merveilleux does not serve standard dishes, but has a kind of 'try-it-and-see' menu, where you get several different flavours and textures on your plate. Interesting.'

» **Pane Pane**, Sint-Jakobsstraat 2, tel. +32 (0)50 49 09 54
'Sometimes you don't want a full lunch but just need a budget-friendly sandwich. If so, this is the place for you. At Pane Pane your oven-fresh sandwiches are prepared right in front of your very own eyes by Gracienne and Jojo, the sweetest ladies in all Bruges.'

CAFÉS

» **Bar Salon**, Langestraat 17,
  www.rock-fort.be

'Inventive mini-dishes, original tapas and some traditional cocktail classics, all served in an adventurous contemporary interior. That is Bar Salon, a place where you can first order some excellent *jamon iberico*, followed perhaps by tuna tartare or some *pan con tomate*.'

» **Wijnbar Est**, Braambergstraat 7, tel. +32 (0)50 33 38 39, www.wijnbarest.be
'Noëlla and Marnix serve a fine selection of wines from around the world, by the glass or by the bottle, and they do it in a tiny – and seemingly ancient – house. Tiny? The two floors have just 10 tables in all! Even so, there is still space enough for live music on Sundays.'

» **Groot Vlaenderen**, Vlamingstraat 94, tel. +32 (0)50 68 43 56,
www.grootvlaenderen.be

'A hotel bar, but without the hotel. This fancy new cocktail bar is the only place in Bruges where you can get a perfect Long Island Tea. Arne makes cocktails like the true professional he is, and is also an inspirational entrepreneur. I have great respect for his ambition.'

» **Punta Est**, Predikherenrei 1, tel. +32 (0)50 34 94 10, www.puntaest.be

'Undoubtedly the best sun terrace in Bruges. Away from all the tourist hustle and bustle, but still slap-bang in the middle of the city, with a really great view. The terrace is pleasantly sheltered out of the wind – but don't forget your sun-cream!'

» **De Republiek**, Sint-Jakobsstraat 36, tel. +32 (0)50 34 02 29,
www.derepubliek.be

'De Republiek is probably the nearest thing in Bruges to the traditional 'grand café'. In the morning you can read your paper here; later in the day you might stop by for a coffee's or perhaps an aperitif in the early evening. Of course, you can always eat here. In short, a place where it is fun just to hang out. And in the summer, you can enjoy the sun in the huge interior courtyard.'

SHOPPING LIST

» **Patisserie Academie**, Academiestraat 4, tel. +32 (0)50 68 92 91,
www.patisserieacademie.be

Tom Van Loock learned the confectioner's trade at no less a place than De Karmeliet (good for 3 Michelin stars). He now runs his own patisserie, a little temple of pleasure where only perfection is good enough. The cakes look so delicious that you want to eat them right outside on the pavement.'

» **Dille & Kamille**, Simon Stevinplein 17-18, tel. +32 (0)50 34 11 80,
www.dille-kamille.be

'A fantastic array of kitchen utensils at fantastically-low prices. Here you will find everything you need to bake, roast, fry, poach and… eat! Stylish but affordable. I can never leave without buying something.'

» **De Olijfboom**, Smedenstraat 58, tel. +32 (0)50 34 16 39,
www.deolijfboom.be

'In De Olijfboom you can find 80 different types of olive oil: 12 oils on tap, 2 *novella's* (very young oils from recently harvested olives), 20 flavoured oils (from pistachio through walnut to sesame seed), 50 kinds of vinegar and 20 types of balsamico. Add to this numerous herbs, spices and a fine selection of salts, and you can understand why it is sometimes difficult to choose what to buy.'

» **Exceller Bikes**, Philipstockstraat 43, tel. +32 (0)50 70 68 12,
www.excellerbikes.com

'In this shop you don't just buy a bike. You buy a piece of biking culture. Exceller Bikes promotes a cycling life-style. In fact, the shop is more a kind of *'museum of modern biking'*. A museum full of wonderful bikes, but without all the other (often hideous) cycling paraphernalia...'

» **Oil & Vinegar**, Geldmuntstraat 11, +32 (0)50 34 56 50, www.oilvinegar.com

'Another great foodie address, again right in the middle of town. Here you can buy all different kinds of oils, vinegars, sauces and dressings. And for a unique, personalized present, why not try one of their gift baskets: you decide exactly what goes in it. But be careful – everything in this shop is highly addictive!'

SECRET TIP

'Plan your visit to Bruges for a period when some of the year's major events are organized. This will allow you to enjoy the unique atmosphere of Bruges to the full. If your stay coincides with **KookEet**, the Cactus Festival or the Procession of the Holy Blood, your city trip will be even more unforgettable.'

(For more information about the events in Bruges, see pages 94-97)

Lissewege

Excursions and day trips from Bruges

Lissewege

Time in Lissewege seems to move just that tad slower. With its picturesque canal, whitewashed polder houses and extensive fields and meadows this polder village is a classic example of how every Flemish village once looked: lively, charming and a touch nostalgic.

Onze-Lieve-Vrouw-Bezoek-ingskerk (Our Lady of the Visitation Church) Lissewege

This impressive brick church was erected in an early Gothic style in the 13th century. The remarkable interior counts amongst its treasures a miraculous statue of the Virgin Mary (1625), a striking organ-case and an equally stunning rood loft and pulpit (1652). A truly great attraction is the monumental church tower. The top offers a magnificent panoramic view of the polders.

OPENING TIMES > The church: daily, 10.00 a.m.-5.00 p.m. In summer 9.00 a.m.-8.00 p.m.; the tower: 15/6-30/6 and 1/9-15/9: Saturday and Sunday: 2.30 p.m.-5.00 p.m.; 1/7-31/8: daily: 2.30 p.m.-5.00 p.m.

ADMISSION > Church: free; tower: € 1.00; children under 12: € 0.50

INFORMATION > Onder de Toren, Lissewege, tel. +32 (0)50 54 45 44 (church), tel. +32 (0)50 54 54 72 & +32 (0)487 49 92 14 (tower), www.lissewege.be

Bezoekerscentrum (Visitors Centre) Lissewege

The visitors centre traces the one thousand-year-old history of this white village by way of unique photos, maps, models, paintings and a collection of archaeological finds from the erstwhile Cistercian Abbey of Ter Doest. At the 'Heiligenmuseum' (Museum of Saints) a unique collection of over 100 antique statues of patron saints is on display.

OPENING TIMES > during the Easter holidays and in the period 15/6-15/9: daily 2.00 p.m.-5.30 p.m.; Whit weekend and Ascension weekend, 21/9, 22/9, 28/9 and 29/9 open 2.00 p.m.-5.30 p.m.

ADMISSION > Museum of Saints (+ coffee/tea): € 3.00; Children aged to 11: € 1.00

INFORMATION > Oude Pastoriestraat 5, Lissewege, tel. +32 (0)50 55 29 55, www.lissewege.be

Abdijschuur (Abbey Barn) Ter Doest

The commanding early Gothic abbey barn (13th century) of this former 12th century Cistercian abbey was completely restored early 2000. The dovecote (1651) and monumental gatehouse (1662) have also withstood the ravages of time brilliantly.

OPENING TIMES > Daily 10.00 a.m.-5.00 p.m.

INFORMATION > Ter Doeststraat 4, Lissewege, www.lissewege.be

Bruges' wet- and woodlands

🏙🐬 Boudewijn Seapark Brugge

A jolly dolphin amusement park chock-a-block with attractions and four different animal performances. The dolphins steal the show at the dolphinarium, the sea lions perform a spectacular show at the open air theatre, and the panoramic aquaramas provide a thrilling underwater view. Kids can play to their heart's content in the indoor play village *Bobo's Indoor*. 2013 sees the 50th anniversary of the park's opening – an event that will be celebrated with a brand-new dolphin show.

OPENING TIMES > The park is open from 30/3-29/9. During the Easter holidays

(1/4-14/4) and weekends in April: 10.00 a.m.-5.00 p.m.; May and June: daily, except Wednesday (although open on Wednesday 1/5!), 10.00 a.m.- 5.00 p.m.; July and August: daily, 10.00 a.m.-6.00 a.m.; September: Wednesday, 12.00 p.m.-6.00 p.m.; Saturday and Sunday, 10.00 a.m.-6.00 p.m. From October to March only Bobo's Indoor and the dolphin shows are open to the public, on Wednesday, Saturday and Sunday and during school holidays: 2.00-6.00 p.m.

ADMISSION > All-in ticket (park, shows, play village): adults older than 12 years: € 24.00; children between 1 metre and 11 years old: € 20.00; children between 85 and 99 centimetres: € 7.00; Pay& Display car park: € 6.50; Brugge City Card: € 15.00

Combi-ticket (Bobo's Indoor and the dolphin show (only in the period October-March): adults (from 12 years): € 17.50 (including drink voucher); children smaller than 85 cm and younger than 12 years: € 15.50.

INFORMATION AND TICKETS > A. De Baeckestraat 12, St.-Michiels, tel. +32 (0)50 38 38 38, www.boudewijnseapark.be. Tickets at the amusement park entrance or at the information office 🛈 't Zand (Concertgebouw). Boudewijn Sea Park is situated just outside the city centre and is connected to the Bicycle Route Network. Bus: nr. 7 & nr. 17 – Stop: Boudewijnpark

Kinderboerderij (Children's Farm) De Zeven Torentjes

This 14th-century farmstead houses a merry working children's farm with a superb recreation area and a gaggle of farmyard animals. The beautifully restored dovecot and the Gothic barn are also worth a visit.

OPENING TIMES > From sunrise to sunset. Cafeteria open from Tuesday to Sunday: 11.30 a.m.-9.00 p.m.

ADMISSION > Free

INFORMATION > Canadaring 41, Assebroek; bus: nr. 2 A.Z. St.-Lucas/Assebroek. Stop: Zeven Torentjes

Municipal Domains Beisbroek, Tudor and Chartreuzinnenbos

These extensive nature reserves ensure hours of walking enjoyment. The vast Beisbroek municipal domain (160 hectares) comprises woods, alleys, pastures and heathland. A signposted trail connects the three areas of the domain. Its nature centre spoils nature lovers with an interactive exhibition and a children's lab. A stone's throw away from Beisbroek is another magnet: the Tudor Municipal Domain. Although the Tudor-style castle catches the eye, its ornamental garden and herb garden are also more than worth the while. The park itself boasts pastures and gigantic deciduous trees. The Chartreuzinnenbos (wood of the Carthusian nuns) links the 40 hectares of the Tudor Domain with the 98 hectares of the Beisbroek Domain.

OPENING TIMES > Domain: daily from sunrise to sunset; Nature centre: daily 2.00 p.m.-5.00 p.m. (except Saturday), Sunday and public holidays 2.00 p.m.-6.00 p.m.; Herb Garden: daily from 1/5

language presentations at the informa-tion offices  Markt (Historium), 't Zand (Concertgebouw) and Stations-plein (Station, railway station).

ADMISSION > € 5.00; youngsters under 18: € 4.00

INFORMATION > Zeeweg 96, Sint-Andries, www.beisbroek.be; bus: nr. 52 Brugge/Gistel/Oostende – nr. 53 Brugge/Jabbeke. Stop: Zeeweg

to 15/10, 2.00 p.m.-5.00 p.m. (closed: Saturday).

ADMISSION > Free

INFORMATION > Zeeweg 96, Sint-Andries; Bus: nr. 52 Brugge/Gistel/Oostende – nr. 53 Brugge/Jabbeke. Stop: Zeeweg

Volkssterrenwacht (Public Observatory) Beisbroek

This public observatory zooms in on the sun, the stars and the planets. Its modern planetarium, interactive exhibition and well-equipped observatory unlock the se-crets of the galaxies. The planet trail that starts at the castle is a clever scale model illustrating the distance between the vari-ous planets: each footstep corresponds to nine million space kilometres.

OPENING TIMES > Information on foreign

Lamme Goedzak (steam wheeler) Damme

The nostalgic river boat Lamme Goedzak plies between Noorweegse Kaai in Bruges and the centre of Damme. A bus takes you from Bruges' railway station or Markt to the river boat's jetty and back.

> 1/4-15/10: departures from Bruges to Damme: daily at 10.00 a.m., 12.00 a.m., 2.00 p.m., 4.00 p.m. and 6.00 p.m.; departures from Damme to Bruges: daily at 9.15 a.m., 11.00 a.m., 1.00 p.m., 3.00 p.m. and 5.20 p.m.

FEE > € 7.00 (one-way ticket) or € 10.00 (return ticket); 65+: € 8.00 (one-way ticket) or € 9.00 (return ticket); children aged 3 to 11: € 5.50 (one-way ticket) or

€ 8.00 (return ticket); Brugge City Card
(return ticket): € 7.50
INFORMATION > Noorweegse Kaai 31,
Brugge, tel. +32 (0)9 233 84 69,
www.bootdamme-brugge.be

Triple Treat Quasimodo tour: the best of Belgium in one day

Take it easy on this English-language
minibus tour, which takes you to a.o. illus-
trious Tilleghem Castle and unique Neo-
Gothic Loppem Castle. Included are a
pleasant stroll through medieval Damme
and a visit to the Gothic abbey barn of Ter
Doest at Lissewege. And what would this
tour be without some delicious waffles,
mouth-watering chocolate and a choice
selection of Belgian country ales?
> Excursions on Monday, Wednesday
and Friday from February to December.
You are collected on 't Zand (Map: C10)
at 9.15 a.m. and brought back at around
5.00 p.m. If requested, you can be collected from your own hotel. Booking
essential.
FEE > € 62.50; youngsters under 26:
€ 52.50; including lunch and entrance
fees; a € 10.00 reduction when booking
the Quasimodo WWI Flanders Fields Tour
INFORMATION > tel. 0800 975 25 or
+32(0)50 37 04 70, www.quasimodo.be

City Tour Damme

City Tour minibuses pick you up on Bruges' market square and drop you off at
Damme. Having sailed back to Bruges
on Lamme Goedzak two hours later,
you will be picked up by the bus at the
jetty and transferred to Markt, Bruges'
central square.
> Excursions: April-September, daily
at 4.00 p.m., commentary in French,
Italian, Dutch, English, German and
Spanish.

FEE > € 25.00; children aged 6 to 11: € 17.00

INFORMATION > tel. +32 (0) 50 35 50 24 or info@citytour.be, www.citytour.be

🏛 Uilenspiegelmuseum Damme

Would you like to know more about Tijl Uilenspiegel and his pranks and tomfoolery? And would you like to meet his clones from all over the world and understand the cultural-historical context of this capricious figure? Then Damme is your destination. Here you will not only shake hands with the famous Flemish Uilenspiegel from the 19th century, but also with his 16th-century German colleague and his various 20th-century brothers.

OPENING TIMES > 16/4-15/10: weekdays 9.00 a.m.-12.00 a.m. and 2.00 p.m.-6.00 p.m.; Saturday, Sunday and public

holidays 10.00 a.m.-12.00 a.m. and 2.00 p.m.-6.00 p.m.; 16/10-15/4: weekdays 9.00 a.m.-12.00 a.m. and 2.00 p.m.-5.00 p.m.; Saturday, Sunday and public holidays 2.00 p.m.-5.00 p.m.

ADDITIONAL CLOSING DATES > 1/1 and 25/12

ADMISSION > € 2.50; family ticket: € 5.00; students: € 1.50; Brugge City Card: € 1.50

INFORMATION > Jacob van Maerlantstraat 3, Damme, tel. +32 (0)50 28 86 10, www.toerismedamme.be

🏛 Sint-Janshospitaal (Saint John's Hospital) Damme

Thirteenth-century Saint John's Hospital possesses an impressive collection of liturgical objects and an interesting selection of unusual furniture, paintings and earthenware. The hospital's chapel is open to visitors except during services. Why not kill two birds with one stone and discover not only this fine collection but also the special place where the objects belonged and where they were once used on a daily basis?

OPENING TIMES > Easter to 30/9: 11.00 a.m.-12.00 a.m. and 2.00 p.m.-5.30 p.m.

ADDITIONAL CLOSING DATES > Monday morning and Friday morning, annual closure from 1/10 to 31/3

ADMISSION > € 1.50; family ticket: € 3.00; 65+ and disabled persons: € 1.00; Brugge City Card: € 1.00

INFORMATION > Kerkstraat 33, Damme, tel. +32 (0)50 46 10 80, www.ocmw-damme.be

🏙 Mu.ZEE
Permekemuseum Jabbeke

Constant Permeke, the most famous Flemish expressionist painter, lived and worked in Jabbeke for more than twenty years. His abode was the The Four Winds, a striking villa commissioned by the artist himself and built, for its time, in extremely modern design. Today it is the location of the Permeke Museum, where the visitor can wander around the artist's living quarters as well as his garden and former studios. It is without a doubt the place par excellence to admire in total peace and quiet Permeke's collection of his spellbinding works.

OPENING TIMES > Tuesday to Sunday: 10.00 a.m.-12.30 a.m. and 1.30 p.m.-6.00 p.m. (till 5.30 p.m. from 1/10 to 31/3)

ADDITIONAL CLOSING DATES > Monday; 1/1 and 25/12

ADMISSION > € 3.00; 55+: € 2.50; youngsters under 26: € 1.00; children under 13: free; Brugge City Card: € 2.25

INFORMATION > Gistelsteenweg 341, Jabbeke, tel. +32 (0)59 50 81 18 (Mu.ZEE – Art Museum at the sea), www.muzee.be

▦ Romeins Archeologisch Museum (RAM, Roman Archaeological Museum) Oudenburg

After years of trudging through mud, painstaking excavations and studies, Oudenburg today possesses a unique collection of archaeological artefacts from Roman times. The good news is that the visitor can pore over them at the modernised museum. The reconstructions, scale-models, archaeological finds and computer simulations enable you to get to grips with the region's rich Roman history in a professional way. The adjacent visitor centre brings you also up to date with the Abbey of Saint Peter's, Saint Arnold and the other attractions of this region.

OPENING TIMES > Tuesday to Saturday: 10.00 a.m.-12.30 a.m. and 1.30 p.m.-5.30 p.m., Sunday 2.00 p.m.-5.30 p.m.

ADDITIONAL CLOSING DATES > Annual closure: 1/11-31/3

ADMISSION > Visitor Centre: free; museum: € 5.00; children and youngsters between 7 and 18: € 2.00; students: € 2.00; children under 6 (accompanied by an adult): free, disabled persons: € 3.00; Brugge City Card: € 3.00

INFORMATION > Weststraat 24, Oudenburg, tel. +32 (0)59 56 84 00, www.ram-oudenburg.be

▦ Kasteel (Castle) Wijnendale

A superb moated castle in the Torhout woods. Hours of walking pleasure guaranteed. There is more: at the castle museum the visitor makes a voyage through a thousand-year-old history by means of contemporary presentations, touchscreens and a portable video guide. Witness for example Mary of Burgundy's fall from her horse and watch how King Leopold III of the Belgians surrendered to the Germans on 28 May 1940. And why don't you drop in on the former porter's lodge? It now houses a visitor's centre where you can find everything you always wanted to know about Torhout, the Bruges wet- and woodlands, regional products, rambles, bicycle tours and so on and so forth.

OPENING TIMES > 1/4-30/9: 1.30 p.m.-5.30 p.m. April, May, June: Wednesday,

Saturday and Sunday; July and August: daily, public holidays included; September: Wednesday and Sunday

ADDITIONAL CLOSING DATES >
April to August: first Saturday of the month

ADMISSION > including video guide (pda): € 5.00; children between 3 and 12: € 1.00; Brugge City Card: € 3.00

INFORMATION > Oostendestraat 390, Torhout, tel. +32 (0)50 22 07 70, www. toerismetorhout.be. Public transport: train Brugge – Kortrijk or bus route 62A (Oostende – Torhout)

and 1.30 p.m.-5.00 p.m.; from 15/5 to 15/9 open daily (also during the weekends and on holidays): 9.30 a.m-12.30 p.m. and 1.30 p.m.-5.30 p.m.

ADDITIONAL CLOSING DATES > 16/9-14/5: Monday morning; annual closure: 1/1-2/1, 25/12-31/12

ADMISSION > € 1.50, children between 3 and 12: € 0.50; Brugge City Card: € 1.00

INFORMATION > Ravenhofstraat 5, Torhout, tel. +32 (0)50 22 07 70, www.toerismetorhout.be. Public transport: train Brugge-Kortrijk

Museum Torhouts Aardewerk (Torhout Pottery Museum) Torhout

Pottery from Torhout used to be exported throughout the Western world until the Second World War. Unique pottery creations from the 16th to the 20th-century highlight the rich tradition of this almost lost artistic craft. A splendid illustration of typical Flemish folk art influenced by a.o. Art Deco and Art Nouveau.

OPENING TIMES > from 16/9 to 14/5: Monday to Friday: 9.30 a.m-12.30 p.m.

Zeebrugge

Zeebrugge is much more than a seaport of stature. It is also a pleasant seaside resort with an extensive beach, bathing in an informal holiday atmosphere and boasting a fashionable marina as well as authentic fishermen's districts with genuine fishermen's pubs. In short, the entire world has a rendezvous in Zeebrugge. In addition, the town is both on the Coastal Bicycle Route Network that connects all Flemish seaside resorts and the Bruges' wet- and woodlands Bicycle Route Network.

Harbour Round Trip Zeebrugge

The round trip departs from the old fishing port on board of 'Zephira', a brand-new passenger ship, and sails past the naval base, the Pierre Vandamme Lock (one of the largest in the world), the LNG terminal, the wind farm park, Stern Island and the cruise ships and dredgers. All the time gigantic con-

tainer ships are being loaded and un-loaded along the quays. An experience that offers a unique insight into the harbour and its manifold activities.
> 1/4-14/10: weekends and public holidays, 2.00 p.m.; July and August: daily at 2.00 p.m. and 4.00 p.m. 1/8-19/8: daily extra round trip at 11.00 a.m. Saturday

evening in July and August: harbour round trip followed by a barbecue.
ADMISSION > € 10.00; 60+: € 9.00; children between 3 and 11: € 7.00; Brugge City Card: € 7.50; harbour trip + barbecue: € 30.00
INFORMATION > Embarkation at Jacques Brelsteiger, Tijdokstraat (Old Fishing Port), Zeebrugge, tel. 32 (0)59 70 62 94, www.havenrondvaarten.be

The Beach at Zeebrugge

In winter this is the place par excellence to get a breath of fresh air. In summer the townspeople of Bruges flock to this wide and safe sandy strip to sunbathe, swim and potter about. And why not take a

train to the beach? It's a piece of cake! Adjacent to the beach is the summer railway station.

Seafront Zeebrugge

This maritime theme park in the old fish market plunges the visitor in the harsh world of the fishermen, the history of Zeebrugge's port and life below the sea. Children will enjoy the Russian submarine Foxtrot, the lightship West-Hinder and the brand-new pirates' paradise.

OPENING TIMES > Daily 10.00 a.m.-5.00 p.m.; July and August 10.00 a.m.-6.00 p.m.

ADDITIONAL CLOSING DATES > 1/1 and 25/12, annual closure check website

ADMISSION > € 12.50; children up to 1 metre (accompanied by parent): free; children under 13: € 9.00; 60+ and students: € 11.00; Brugge City Card: € 8.50

INFORMATION > Vismijnstraat 7, Zeebrugge, tel. +32 (0)50 55 14 15, www.seafront.be

A trip to the seaside

🏛 Mu.ZEE Ostend

Mu.ZEE, which houses a unique collection of Belgian art from 1830 onwards, is undoubtedly one of the jewels in the Flemish museum crown: work by James Ensor, Léon Spilliaert, Constant Permeke, Jean Brusselmans, Raoul de Keyzer, Roger Raveel, Panamarenko, Luc Tuymans and many more is permanently on view. The children's section allows your offspring to have a go at art in a playful way. It's child's play, as a matter of fact! And why not drop in on one of the great, high-profiled exhibitions? I bet you won't know where to look first!

OPENING TIMES > Tuesday to Sunday: 10.00 a.m.-6.00 p.m.

ADDITIONAL CLOSING DATES > Monday; 1/1 and 25/12
ADMISSION > Permanent collection: € 5.00; 55+: € 4.00; youngsters under 26: € 1.00; children under 13: free; entrance fees are increased for exhibitions; Brugge City Card: € 3.75 (permanent collection)
INFORMATION > Romestraat 11, Oostende, tel. +32 (0)59 50 81 18, www.mu zee.be, public transport: Buses 6 and 14

🏛 Mu.ZEE Ensorhuis (Ensorhouse) Ostend

Oostende is your destination if you want to wander through the mind of James Ensor (1860-1949). This house was indeed the operating base of the world-famous

painter from 1917 onwards. The sea-shell and souvenir shop of his aunt and uncle on the ground-floor has been preserved in its original state. The first floor is occupied by the Blue Salon, where Ensor lived and worked. On the first floor landing so-called 'case-file' exhibitions are regularly held. But people who are hoping to see real works by the master will be disappointed: this small museum only contains reproductions. Even so, the Ensor House offers a fascinating journey back into the world of the early 20th century – and into the mind of a truly great artist.

OPENING TIMES > Wednesday to Monday: 10.00 a.m.-12.00 a.m. and 2.00 p.m.-5.00 p.m.

ADDITIONAL CLOSING DATES >
Tuesday; 1/1 and 25/12

ADMISSION > € 2.00; 55+ and youngsters under 26: € 1.00; children under 12: free; Brugge City Card: € 1.50

INFORMATION > Vlaanderenstraat 27, Oostende, tel. +32 (0)59 50 33 37 (reception) or +32 (0) 497 59 55 76, www.muzee.be. Public transport: Centrumbus (Stop at Vlaanderenstraat), coast tram (Stop at Marie-Joséplein)

Battlefields: Flanders and the Great War

Quasimodo WWI Flanders Fields Tour

Quasimodo takes you on a personalised and relaxing minibus tour to all the highlights: Passchendaele, Hill 60, Messines Ridge, several cemeteries (Commonwealth and German), trenches and bunkers, the Menin Gate and various ANZAC, Canadian, British and Irish monuments. Our stories bring four years of terrible warfare in the Ypres Salient back to life.

OPENING TIMES > February to the end of December: daily except Monday. You are collected on 't Zand (Map: C10) at 9.15 a.m. and brought back at around 5.30 p.m. If requested, you can be collected at your own hotel. Booking essential.

ADMISSION > English spoken: € 62.50; youngsters under 26: € 52.50; tour includes lunch and admission fees; a € 10.00 reduction when booking the Triple Treat Quasimodo Tour: The best of Belgium in one day.

INFORMATION > tel. 0800 975 25 or +32 (0)50 37 04 70, www.quasimodo.be

Flanders Fields Battlefield Daytours

Discover the tourist attractions of the Westhoek and the Great War. Visit the German cemetery at Langemark, Tyne Cot Cemetery and Passchendaele, the Passchendaele Museum with its 'dugout tunnel experience', the Menin Gate, Ypres with her magnificent clothmakers' hall and the must see *In Flanders Fields Museum*. The trip also takes in Hill 62, Hill 60 with its craters and bunkers, Heuvelland and Mount Kemmel, Messines ridge, mine craters 1917, trenches and various other monuments.

OPENING TIMES > Tuesday to Sunday: departure at 8.45 a.m. You are collected from your own hotel. The tour finishes at 5.15 p.m. Booking essential. English, Dutch and French commentary.

ADMISSION (daytrip) > € 65.00; youngsters under 26: € 60.00; includes lunch (no picnic); special Day Tour on request (tailor-made). The Last Post Tour is a short evening trip to Ypres and back to see the Last Post ceremony at the Menin Gate. Departure 6.15 p.m. The tour finishes at 9.15 p.m. Booking essential. English, Dutch and French commentary.

ADMISSION (evening trip) > € 40.00
INFORMATION > tel. 0800 99 133 or +32 (0)50 34 60 60, www.visitbruges.org

In Flanders Fields Museum Ypres

Welcome to this recently updated and highly interactive museum, which offers

a fascinating and memorable interpretation of the events of the Great War. This is no dry summary of facts and figures, but a truly participative experience that uses modern techniques, sound effects and authentic film images to retell the history of the war in a manner that will leave no one unmoved. It is almost as if you are standing in the trenches yourself or watching the city of Ieper being destroyed with your very own eyes. Every visitor is given a personalised poppy armband, which allows you to choose your own preferred language and also gives access the personal histories of four participants in the war, whose stories are then followed throughout the museum trajectory. In short, this is a museum that you must experience before you can actually believe it!

OPENING TIMES > 1/4-15/11: daily from 10.00 a.m.-6.00 p.m.; 16/11-31/3: from Tuesday to Sunday, from 10.00 a.m.-5.00 p.m. (last ticket sale one hour before closure).

ADDITIONAL CLOSING DATES > 1/1, 25/12, and the three weeks following the Belgian Christmas holiday

ADMISSION > € 8.00; youngsters between 7 and 25: € 1.00; children under 7: free; Brugge City Card: € 5.50

INFORMATION > Grote Markt 34, Ieper, tel. +32 (0)57 23 92 20, www.inflandersfields.be

Canada-Poland War Museum Adegem

If you want to be put in the picture of Flanders during the Second World War, then the Canada-Poland War Museum is the place to be. A large number of life-like tableaux showing a.o. the Battle of the Leopold Canal and a vast collection of photographs, weapons, radio-transmitters and uniforms give an excellent insight into the war years. Children will be able to experience at eye level 'The Second World War in miniature', a display of all the battles on a 1/35 scale.

OPENING TIMES > April to September: Tuesday to Sunday, 10.00 a.m.-6.00 p.m.; October to March: Wednesday to Sunday, 12.00 a.m.-6.00 p.m.

ADDITIONAL CLOSING DATES > 1/1, annual closure: one week in October (check the website)

ADMISSION > € 5.00; children under 7: free; Brugge City Card: € 4.00, picture postcard included or € 7.00 for both museums (Canada and Poland Museum)

INFORMATION > Heulendonk 21, Adegem, tel. +32 (0)50 71 06 66, www.canadamuseum.be

Other places of interest

⬛ Centrum Ronde van Vlaanderen (Tour of Flanders Centre) Oudenaarde

The multi-medial Tour of Flanders Centre, in the heart of the Flemish Ardennes, is a multi-media museum with many different facets – all of them interesting! There is an interactive experience museum, an exhibition area, a film auditorium and the fun 'Tour Shop'. Last but definitely not least, there is also the Bikers Brasserie! The museum leads visitors through the history and traditions of Flanders' greatest cycling race, which is burnt into the soul of the Flemish people. Thanks to the use of multi-media magic, you can actually take part in the race yourself. Test out Tom Boonen's bike, specially designed to cope with the race's cobbled stretches, or sweat your way to the top of the Oude Kwaremont hill in the wheel of Peter Van Petegem. And once you have crossed the finishing line,

mount the podium as winner of 'Flanders' Finest'. The friendly and helpful staff at the entrance desk will tell you everything you want to know about other tourist attractions and cycling routes in the Flemish Ardennes. Tired cyclists can even take a refreshing shower here if they want to!

OPENING TIMES > Tuesday to Sunday: 10.00 a.m.-6.00 p.m.

ADDITIONAL CLOSING DATES > 1/1, from 7/1 to 20/1, 25/12

ADMISSION > € 8.00; 60+ € 6.00; students and children under 15: € 4.00; family ticket (2 adults and 4 children max.): € 17.50; Brugge City Card: € 6.00; 60+: € 4,00; students and children under 15: € 3,00; family ticket: € 12,50

INFORMATION > Markt 43, Oudenaarde, tel. +32 (0)55 33 99 33, www.crvv.be, public transport: a bus links Oudenaarde railway station (on the Ghent-Sint-Pieters to Ronse line) with Markt

Index of street names